Barcelona: A Guide for All Seasons.

How to enjoy the city in any weather, with recommendations on what to pack, what to wear, and what to do.

By: Dane Joe

Contents

My personal Barcelona experience.

Location: El Xampanyet, Barcelona

Date: July 15, 2022

Description: One of the most unforgettable moments during my trip to Barcelona was when I stumbled upon El Xampanyet, a charming tapas bar nestled in the historic El Born neighborhood. The rustic interior, with its wooden barrels and authentic Catalan decor, transported me to another time. As I sat at the crowded bar, I was instantly welcomed by the lively atmosphere and the tantalizing aromas of traditional Spanish dishes.

I ordered a variety of tapas, from crispy patatas bravas to succulent grilled prawns, and each bite was a burst of flavor that left me craving more. The star of the show was the house specialty, "xampanyet," a sparkling wine served in ice-cold glasses, which perfectly complemented the savory dishes.

The friendly locals and fellow travelers at the bar made it easy to strike up conversations and exchange travel tips, creating a warm and inclusive environment. I spent hours savoring tapas, sipping xampanyet, and making new friends, which turned this impromptu visit into an authentic Barcelona experience I'll never forget.

Recommendations: El Xampanyet can get quite busy, so try to visit during off-peak hours or be prepared to wait a little for a spot at the bar. It's an ideal place for solo travelers looking to meet people and for food enthusiasts eager to taste some of the best tapas in Barcelona.

Memorable Moments: The moment I took my first bite of patatas bravas and felt the fizzy burst of xampanyet on my palate, I knew I had found a hidden gem in Barcelona. The camaraderie with locals and fellow travelers added to the magic of this experience.Overall

Impression: El Xampanyet offers an authentic taste of Barcelona's culinary scene and the opportunity to immerse yourself in the local culture. It's a must-visit for food lovers and anyone seeking a genuine and welcoming atmosphere in the heart of the city.

Rating: ★★★★★

Your Name: [Dane Joe]

1. Introduction to Barcelona

  - Brief overview of Barcelona

Barcelona is a beautiful and vibrant city in the northeastern coast of Spain. It is the capital of Catalonia, a region with its own language, culture, and history. Barcelona has a rich and diverse heritage, from its Roman origins to its modernist architecture. Here are some facts about Barcelona that you might find interesting:

- Barcelona is the second-most populous city in Spain, with about 1.6 million people living within its city limits. Its urban area extends to many neighbouring municipalities and has a population of about 4.8 million people.

- Barcelona is one of the most popular tourist destinations in Europe, attracting millions of visitors every year. Some of the most famous attractions include the Sagrada Familia, a stunning basilica designed by Antoni Gaudí; the Picasso Museum, which houses one of the largest collections of the artist's works; and Las Ramblas, a lively boulevard full of shops, cafes, and street performers.

- Barcelona is also a major cultural, economic, and financial centre in southwestern Europe. It is the main biotech hub in Spain and hosts many international events and conferences. It is also home to two prestigious universities: the University of Barcelona and Pompeu Fabra University.

- Barcelona has a Mediterranean climate, with mild winters and warm summers. The average temperature ranges from 10°C in January to 25°C in August. The city enjoys about 300 days of sunshine per year and receives about 640 mm of rainfall annually.

- Barcelona has a strong sporting tradition, especially in football (soccer). The city's main team, FC Barcelona, is one of the most successful and popular clubs in the world, with millions of fans around the globe. The club's motto is "Més que un club" (More than a club), reflecting its social and cultural role in Catalonia. Barcelona also hosted the 1992 Summer Olympics, which boosted its international reputation and urban development.

- Why visit Barcelona?
Barcelona is a wonderful city to visit for many reasons. It is a place where you can enjoy the beauty of art, nature, culture, and cuisine. Here are some of the reasons why you should visit Barcelona:

- Barcelona has some of the most stunning and unique architecture in the world, thanks to the genius of Antoni Gaudí. His masterpieces, such as the Sagrada Família, Casa Batlló, Park Güell, and La Pedrera, are UNESCO World Heritage Sites and attract millions of visitors every year. You will be amazed by the creativity and originality of his designs, which blend organic forms, vibrant colors, and symbolic elements.

- Barcelona is a city full of life and energy, especially on its main street, Las Ramblas. This is a long boulevard that connects the Plaça de Catalunya with the port, and it is always crowded with people, shops, cafes, and street performers. You can stroll along Las Ramblas and enjoy the lively atmosphere, or stop by the famous La Boquería market, where you can find fresh produce, seafood, cheese, ham, and other delicacies.

- Barcelona is a great destination for food lovers, as it offers a variety of dishes that reflect the rich and diverse Catalan cuisine. You can sample some of the traditional tapas, such as patatas bravas, croquetas, tortilla de patatas, pan con tomate, and jamón ibérico. You can also try some of the regional specialties, such as paella, fideuà, escalivada, esqueixada, crema catalana, and cava.

- Barcelona is a city with a strong cultural identity and heritage, which you can discover through its museums, galleries, festivals, and traditions. You can visit some of the world-class museums that showcase the works of famous artists such as Picasso, Dalí, Miró, and Tàpies. You can also experience some of the local festivals that celebrate Catalan history and culture, such as La Mercè, Sant Jordi, Sant Joan, and La Diada. You can also witness some of the unique traditions that are part of the UNESCO Intangible Cultural Heritage of Humanity, such as the castellers (human towers), the sardana (folk dance), and the correfoc (fire run).

- Barcelona is a city that offers both urban and natural attractions, as it is located between the sea and the mountains. You can enjoy the sunny weather and relax on one of the many beaches that line the Mediterranean coast. You can also explore some of the green spaces that surround the city, such as Montjuïc hill, Collserola park, or Tibidabo mountain. You can also take advantage of the proximity to other beautiful places in Catalonia, such as Montserrat monastery, Sitges town, or Costa Brava coast.

These are just some of the reasons why you should visit Barcelona at least once in your lifetime. There is so much more to see and do in this amazing city that you will never get bored or run out of options. I hope this has inspired you to plan your trip to Barcelona soon! ●

2. Getting There

- How to reach Barcelona

Here's an extensive note on how to reach Barcelona, Spain:

How to Reach Barcelona, Spain: Transportation Options

Barcelona, the vibrant capital of Catalonia, is a popular destination for tourists and business travelers alike. Reaching this beautiful city can be done through various transportation options, each offering its own advantages. Below, we'll explore the different ways to reach Barcelona:

1. By Air (Flight):
   - Barcelona-El Prat Airport (BCN): The most common way to reach Barcelona is by air. Barcelona-El Prat Airport, located just 12 kilometers from the city center, is the main international gateway. It's well-connected to major cities worldwide. You can book direct flights to BCN from many international destinations.

2. By Train:
   - High-Speed Trains: Barcelona has an extensive and efficient railway network. You can opt for high-speed trains, such as the AVE, which connects major Spanish cities like Madrid, Valencia, and Seville to Barcelona. The TGV also connects Barcelona to France, including cities like Paris.

- Regional Trains: If you're traveling from nearby cities within Catalonia or other regions of Spain, regional trains are available. These may be a more budget-friendly option.

3. By Bus:
   - Long-Distance Buses: Various long-distance bus companies, including ALSA and FlixBus, provide bus services to Barcelona. This option is often more economical and can be convenient if you're traveling from other Spanish cities or European destinations. The main bus terminal in Barcelona is Estació del Nord.

4. By Car:
   - Driving to Barcelona: For those who prefer the flexibility of a road trip, you can drive to Barcelona. However, be prepared for city traffic and parking challenges. Make sure you're familiar with local traffic rules and have a plan for parking your vehicle. Barcelona is well-connected to the European road network via highways like the AP-7 and AP-2.

5. By Sea:
   - Ferry Services: If you're arriving from Mediterranean destinations or nearby coastal areas, consider taking a ferry. Barcelona's port is a popular stop for ferry services, connecting the city to the Balearic Islands, Italy, and other Mediterranean ports.

6. Cruise Travel:

- Cruise Ships: If you're on a cruise vacation, Barcelona is often included as a port of call. You can disembark at the city's port, which is conveniently located near many of the city's attractions.

Before planning your trip, remember to check for the most up-to-date travel information, including any entry requirements, visa regulations, COVID-19 restrictions, and other considerations. Transportation options may change, so it's important to verify the latest details and book your travel accordingly. Barcelona awaits with its rich history, stunning architecture, delicious cuisine, and beautiful beaches, making it a captivating destination for travelers.

3. Accommodation.

- Types of accommodations (Hotels, Hostels, Airbnb etc.)

Let's explore the types of accommodations in Barcelona in detail:

1. Hotels:

- Luxury Hotels: Barcelona is home to several world-class luxury hotels that offer exceptional service, stunning views, and top-notch amenities. Examples include Hotel Arts, renowned for its exquisite dining and spa, and W Barcelona, with its iconic sail-shaped structure and beachfront location.

- Boutique Hotels: Boutique hotels in Barcelona often occupy historic or uniquely designed buildings. They provide an intimate atmosphere, personalized service, and stylish decor. Consider staying at Hotel Casa Fuster, an Art Nouveau gem, or Hotel Neri, nestled in the heart of the Gothic Quarter.

- Mid-Range Hotels: Mid-range hotels cater to travelers seeking a balance between comfort and affordability. These establishments offer well-appointed rooms, friendly service, and convenient locations across the city.

- Budget Hotels: If you're on a tighter budget, Barcelona has a range of budget-friendly hotels that offer the basics for a comfortable stay without breaking the bank.

2. Hostels:
 - Youth Hostels: Barcelona's youth hostels provide affordable accommodation for backpackers and budget-conscious travelers. You can expect dormitory-style rooms, communal spaces for socializing, and organized activities. Popular options include Kabul Hostel and Sant Jordi Hostels.

3. Vacation Rentals:
 - Airbnb: Airbnb offers a wide range of vacation rentals in Barcelona, from cozy apartments in the Eixample district to beachfront villas in Sitges. These provide the flexibility of self-catering and a more home-like atmosphere.
 - Vrbo and HomeAway: Similar to Airbnb, Vrbo and HomeAway offer a variety of vacation rental options, including houses, condos, and more.

4. Guesthouses and Bed and Breakfasts:
 - Barcelona has numerous guesthouses and bed and breakfasts, often found in charming historic buildings. These accommodations offer a cozy and intimate atmosphere, with personalized service and local recommendations.

5. Pensions and Hostals:
 - Pensions and hostals are small, family-run accommodations that may be located in older buildings. They are typically budget-friendly and offer a more authentic, local experience. Some may have basic

facilities, but they often have a warm and welcoming atmosphere.

6. Resorts (in nearby coastal areas):
   - While Barcelona is primarily known for its city attractions, there are beach resorts in nearby coastal towns such as Sitges and the Costa Brava. These resorts offer beachfront relaxation, water sports, and resort amenities.

7. Student Accommodations (dormitory-style options):
   - Some universities in Barcelona offer dormitory-style accommodations to visitors, especially during academic breaks. This can be a cost-effective choice for students and budget travelers.

8. Campsites (located in the outskirts of the city):
   - Camping enthusiasts can explore campsites on the outskirts of Barcelona. These sites often include facilities like swimming pools and access to natural areas, offering an outdoor experience within reach of the city.

When choosing your accommodation in Barcelona, consider factors such as location, budget, the type of experience you desire, and the amenities you need. Reservations are advisable, particularly during the peak tourist season, to secure the best options. Barcelona's accommodations cater to a wide range of travelers, making it a welcoming destination for all.

   - Popular neighborhoods to stay in.

Let's explore each of Barcelona's neighborhoods in more detail:

1. Eixample:

- Overview: Eixample, meaning "extension" in Catalan, is one of Barcelona's most iconic districts. It's known for its grid-like layout, Modernist architecture, and wide, elegant avenues.
- Highlights: La Sagrada Família, Casa Batlló, Casa Milà (La Pedrera), and many upscale shops and restaurants.
- Atmosphere: A mix of upscale and residential areas with a cosmopolitan atmosphere.
- Best For: Art and architecture lovers, shoppers, and those looking for a central location.

2. Gothic Quarter (Barri Gòtic):

- Overview: The Gothic Quarter is the historical heart of Barcelona, with medieval buildings, narrow alleys, and picturesque squares.
- Highlights: Barcelona Cathedral, Plaça Reial, Museu d'Història de Barcelona, and the lively La Rambla nearby.
- Atmosphere: An enchanting and historic atmosphere with a vibrant café culture.
- Best For: History and culture enthusiasts, tourists seeking an authentic Barcelona experience.

3. El Raval:
- Overview: El Raval is a dynamic, multicultural neighborhood, known for its diverse population, street art, and emerging arts scene.
- Highlights: MACBA (Museum of Contemporary Art), Centre de Cultura Contemporània de Barcelona (CCCB), and unique bars and eateries.
- Atmosphere: Eclectic and trendy with a vibrant street life.
- Best For: Artsy and alternative travelers, foodies, and those seeking a diverse atmosphere.

4. El born:

- Overview: El Born is a historic district with narrow alleys, medieval architecture, and a lively atmosphere.
- Highlights: Picasso Museum, Santa Maria del Mar, and a thriving restaurant scene.
- Atmosphere: Artsy and charming, with a mix of locals and tourists.
- Best For: Art lovers, history buffs, and food enthusiasts.

5. La Barceloneta:
- Overview: La Barceloneta is Barcelona's beach neighborhood, known for its seafront promenade, sandy shores, and seafood restaurants.
- Highlights: Barceloneta Beach, Barceloneta Market, and waterfront dining.
- Atmosphere: A relaxed, beach-town vibe.
- Best For: Beach lovers, water sports enthusiasts, and those seeking coastal relaxation.

6. Poble Sec:

  - Overview: Poble Sec is an up-and-coming neighborhood known for its arts community and proximity to Montjuïc.

  - Highlights: Montjuïc Park, Poble Espanyol, and a mix of traditional and trendy bars.

  - Atmosphere: Artsy, vibrant, and eclectic.

  - Best For: Arts and culture enthusiasts, outdoor lovers, and those looking for a neighborhood on the rise.

7. Gràcia:

  - Overview: Gràcia is a hip and bohemian neighborhood known for its village-like atmosphere, squares, and unique shops.

  - Highlights: Plaça del Sol, Plaça de la Vila de Gràcia, and a variety of quirky boutiques.

  - Atmosphere: Relaxed, artistic, and community-oriented.

  - Best For: Bohemian travelers, creatives, and those seeking a local experience.

8. Sant Antoni:

   - Overview: Sant Antoni is a traditional neighborhood known for its food market and trendy dining establishments.
   - Highlights: Sant Antoni Market, restaurants, and bars.
   - Atmosphere: A mix of traditional and modern, with a bustling market atmosphere.
   - Best For: Foodies, market lovers, and those looking for local cuisine.

9. Les Corts:
   - Overview: Les Corts is a primarily residential district known for its tranquility and proximity to FC Barcelona's Camp Nou stadium.

- Highlights: Camp Nou Experience, shopping areas like L'illa Diagonal, and local parks.
- Atmosphere: Residential and calm, with a mix of locals and visitors.
- Best For: Sports enthusiasts, shoppers, and travelers seeking a quieter area.

10. Sarrià-Sant Gervasi:

- Overview: Sarrià-Sant Gervasi is an upscale district featuring elegant avenues, high-end boutiques, and gourmet dining.
- Highlights: Park del Putxet, Tibidabo amusement park, designer shopping on Avinguda Diagonal, and renowned restaurants.
- Atmosphere: Elegant and sophisticated, with a suburban feel.
- Best For: Luxury travelers, shoppers, and those who appreciate fine dining.

11. Horta-Guinardó:

- Overview: Horta-Guinardó is a hilly neighborhood with a mix of residential and green spaces, making it a peaceful retreat from the city's hustle and bustle.
- Highlights: Park Güell, Hospital de Sant Pau, and natural parks in the hills.
- Atmosphere: Serene and natural, with pockets of historic charm.
- Best For: Nature lovers, hikers, and travelers looking for a peaceful escape.

12. Sants-Montjuïc:

- Overview: Sants-Montjuïc is a diverse district that encompasses the Montjuïc hill, known for its cultural attractions, parks, and panoramic views.
- Highlights: Montjuïc Castle, Magic Fountain of Montjuïc, Poble Espanyol, and various museums.
- Atmosphere: A blend of cultural and green spaces, with an urban feel in some areas.
- Best For: Cultural explorers, outdoor enthusiasts, and travelers seeking a mix of attractions.

13. Diagonal Mar:

- Overview: Diagonal Mar is a modern and urban neighborhood located near the sea, offering contemporary living and shopping experiences.
- Highlights: Diagonal Mar Shopping Center, Diagonal Mar Park, and proximity to the beach.
- Atmosphere: Modern, sleek, and family-friendly.
- Best For: Shoppers, families, and those who enjoy a modern seaside atmosphere.

Each of these neighborhoods contributes to Barcelona's diverse character. When choosing where to stay, consider the ambiance, attractions, and proximity to your points of interest. Whether you seek the lively atmosphere of the city center, a historic district, a tranquil residential area, or a beachfront escape, Barcelona offers a neighborhood to match your preferences.

4. Getting Around

- Public transportation (Metro, Buses)
Public Transportation in Barcelona: Metro and Buses

Barcelona boasts an extensive and efficient public transportation system, making it easy to explore the city and its surrounding areas. The two primary modes of public transport in Barcelona are the metro (subway) and buses, which are well-connected, affordable, and convenient for both residents and tourists.

Metro:

Overview: The Barcelona Metro is one of the most important elements of the city's public transportation network. It's operated by Transports Metropolitans de Barcelona (TMB) and serves as a backbone for commuting within the city.

Network: The metro network consists of several lines, each marked by a different color, and it covers the entire city. Lines 1 (red), 2 (purple), 3 (green), and 4 (yellow) are the primary lines that crisscross the city, making it easy to access most major attractions.

Frequency: Metro trains typically run from 5:00 AM to midnight. During weekdays, the frequency is every 3-5 minutes during peak hours and every 7-10 minutes during off-peak hours. On weekends, the service may be less frequent.

 Tickets: You can purchase single-ride tickets or use various travel cards, such as the T-10 card (good for ten journeys on the metro or bus) or Hola Barcelona card (provides unlimited travel on public transport for 2, 3, 4, or 5 consecutive days). It's important to validate your ticket upon entering the metro station.

 Accessibility: The Barcelona Metro is wheelchair-accessible, with elevators and ramps in most stations. Trains also have designated spaces for passengers with reduced mobility.

Buses:

 Overview: Buses in Barcelona complement the metro system and offer routes that extend to areas not covered by the subway. They are operated by the TMB and other companies.

 Network: Barcelona's bus network is extensive, with multiple bus lines connecting different parts of the city. The bus routes are often identified by numbers and can take you to neighborhoods, parks, and attractions that may not have direct metro access.

 Frequency: Bus frequency varies depending on the route and the time of day. On major routes, buses can be as frequent as every 5-10 minutes during peak hours.

Tickets: Similar to the metro, you can use single-ride tickets or travel cards that are also valid on the metro. The T-10 card, which offers flexibility and savings, can be used on both metro and buses.

Night Buses: Barcelona operates a network of Nitbus (night bus) services, which run from midnight to 4:00 AM, providing transportation options for night owls and those working late.

Hop-On, Hop-Off Buses: Tourist buses, such as the Barcelona Bus Turístic, are a popular choice for tourists. These hop-on, hop-off buses offer narrated tours with stops at major attractions.

Integrating Metro and Buses:

Both the metro and buses in Barcelona are integrated into the same ticketing system. This means that you can use the same travel card or ticket to access both modes of transport within a specified timeframe. This integration makes it convenient to switch between the metro and buses when navigating the city.

Public transportation in Barcelona is a cost-effective, efficient, and eco-friendly way to explore the city. It's an excellent choice for both tourists and locals, allowing easy access to the city's many attractions, neighborhoods, and cultural sites. Whether you're traveling to the Gothic Quarter, the beach, or one of

Gaudí's masterpieces, the metro and buses are essential tools for your journey through Barcelona.

 - Taxis, Uber
Taxis and Ride-Sharing Services in Barcelona: A Comprehensive Guide

Barcelona, like many major cities, offers a variety of transportation options, including traditional taxis and ride-sharing services such as Uber. Below, we'll delve into each option, outlining their services, availability, and important considerations.

Taxis in Barcelona:

 Services: Traditional taxis are a ubiquitous and reliable mode of transportation in Barcelona. They provide point-to-point service and can be hailed on the street, booked by phone, or found at designated taxi stands.
 Identification: Licensed taxis in Barcelona are usually black and yellow, making them easy to spot. Look for the green light on the taxi's roof, which indicates availability.
 Fares: Taxis in Barcelona are metered, with fares that are regulated by the government. The rates are reasonable, and the meter will display the cost of your journey.
 Payment: Taxis accept both cash and credit cards. You can also tip your driver if you wish, though it's not mandatory.

Accessibility: Most taxis in Barcelona are wheelchair-accessible, but it's advisable to request an accessible taxi in advance.

Pros of Taxis:
- Readily available throughout the city.
- Drivers are typically knowledgeable about the city's layout.
- Regulated fares provide transparency and prevent price fluctuations.

Cons of Taxis:
- Taxis may be harder to find during peak hours or in less crowded areas.
- Language barriers with drivers can occasionally be a challenge.

Uber and Ride-Sharing in Barcelona:

Services: Uber once operated in Barcelona, but as of my last knowledge update in September 2021, it had to suspend its ride-sharing service due to regulatory issues. However, it's important to check the latest updates, as regulations and services can change.
Alternative Ride-Sharing Services: While Uber had challenges in Barcelona, other local and international ride-sharing companies may be available. Be sure to research and confirm the current status and legality of any ride-sharing services operating in the city.

Pros of Ride-Sharing:

- Convenient booking via mobile apps.
- Often provide clear pricing before your journey.
- Can offer a cashless payment option.

Cons of Ride-Sharing:
- Availability can be limited or subject to regulatory changes.
- May not have as extensive a network as traditional taxis.

Important Considerations:

Regulations: It's crucial to stay updated on the current legal status of ride-sharing services in Barcelona, as regulations can change. This applies not only to Uber but also to other similar services.

Language: Communication with drivers can sometimes be challenging if you don't speak Spanish or Catalan. However, many taxi drivers understand basic English.

Payment Methods: Taxis and ride-sharing services typically accept both cash and credit cards. Always confirm payment options with the driver before your journey.

In summary, traditional taxis are a well-established and reliable mode of transportation in Barcelona. While Uber faced regulatory challenges, other ride-sharing options may exist. To ensure a smooth experience, it's essential to stay informed about the current status and regulations governing ride-sharing services in the city. Both options have their merits, and the choice often depends on factors like availability, convenience, and personal preference.

 - Walking and biking
Walking and Biking in Barcelona: A Healthy and Eco-Friendly Way to Explore the City

Walking and biking are fantastic ways to explore Barcelona, as they allow you to fully immerse yourself in the city's culture, history, and stunning architecture. Here's an extensive look at the benefits, routes, and important considerations for walking and biking in Barcelona:

Walking in Barcelona:

 Benefits:
 - Immersive Experience: Walking lets you take in the city's sights, sounds, and smells at a leisurely pace.
 - Healthy and Eco-Friendly: It's an environmentally friendly way to explore, and it's good exercise.
 - Flexibility: You can easily explore narrow alleys, plazas, and hidden gems that may not be accessible by other means.

 Routes:
 - Las Ramblas: Barcelona's most famous street is a pleasant walk, lined with shops, cafes, and street performers.

- Gothic Quarter: Explore the historic heart of the city with its winding alleys, cathedrals, and charming squares.
- Beach Promenade: Stroll along Barceloneta Beach for a refreshing seafront experience.

Considerations:
- Comfortable Shoes: Wear comfortable shoes suitable for walking on cobblestone streets.
- Weather: Be prepared for Barcelona's Mediterranean climate, which can be hot in summer and mild in winter.
- Safety: Watch out for pickpockets, especially in crowded areas. Keep your belongings secure.

Biking in Barcelona:

Benefits:
- Efficient Transportation: Biking allows you to cover more ground and reach attractions quickly.
- Bike Lanes: Barcelona has an expanding network of bike lanes, making it safer for cyclists.
- Rental Options: Numerous bike rental shops and bike-sharing services are available.

Routes:
- Barcelona's Beaches: Cycle along the seafront promenade to enjoy the beach and sea views.
- Montjuïc Hill: Explore Montjuïc's parks and attractions by bike for panoramic views of the city.
- Passeig de Gràcia: Visit Modernist landmarks like Casa Batlló and La Pedrera along this elegant avenue.

Considerations:
  - Safety: Always wear a helmet and follow traffic rules.
Be cautious around pedestrians in shared spaces.
  - Bike Rentals: Look for reputable bike rental shops
with well-maintained bicycles.
  - Locks: Use a sturdy lock to secure your bike when
parking, and be mindful of bike theft.

Integrated Transport:

Barcelona's integrated transport system allows you to
combine walking and biking with other modes of public
transportation. You can take your bike on the metro,
trams, and some buses. This flexibility enhances your
mobility and exploration options.

Whether you prefer leisurely strolls through historic
neighborhoods or zipping around the city on a bike,
walking and biking in Barcelona offer incredible
opportunities to experience the city's beauty and culture.
Just remember to stay safe, follow local regulations, and
enjoy the journey at your own pace.

5. Top Attractions

Let's explore these top attractions in Barcelona in more detail, along with their locations:

1. La Sagrada Família:

 - Location: Carrer de Mallorca, 401, 08013 Barcelona
 - Overview: The Basilica of the Sagrada Família is one of the most recognizable landmarks in Barcelona. Designed by Antoni Gaudí, this awe-inspiring basilica has been under construction since 1882 and is expected to be completed in the coming years.
 - Highlights: The Nativity Façade, the Passion Façade, the Glory Façade, and the breathtaking interior with its forest-like columns.

2. Park Güell:

- Location: Carrer d'Olot, s/n, 08024 Barcelona
- Overview: Park Güell is a public park filled with colorful mosaics, whimsical sculptures, and unique architectural elements, all designed by Antoni Gaudí. It offers a surreal and enchanting experience.
- Highlights: The famous serpentine bench on the main terrace, the iconic dragon fountain, and Gaudí's house.

3. Casa Batlló:
- Location: Passeig de Gràcia, 43, 08007 Barcelona
- Overview: Casa Batlló is another Gaudí masterpiece, known for its undulating facade and colorful, dragon-like rooftop. It's a shining example of modernist architecture.
- Highlights: The rooftop terrace with its dragon-inspired structure, the noble floor (Noble Floor), and the stunning light well.

4. Casa Milà (La Pedrera):

- Location: Carrer de Provença, 261-265, 08008 Barcelona
- Overview: La Pedrera, also known as Casa Milà, is one of Gaudí's most distinctive works, featuring an unconventional design and an undulating roof landscape.
- Highlights: The mesmerizing rooftop terrace, the Espai Gaudí museum, and the interior courtyards.

5. Gothic Quarter (Barri Gòtic):
- Location: Barcelona's historic heart, stretching from La Rambla to Via Laietana
- Overview: The Gothic Quarter is a labyrinth of narrow medieval streets, picturesque plazas, and historic landmarks.
- Highlights: Barcelona Cathedral, Plaça Reial, Plaça del Rei, and the Jewish Quarter (El Call).

6. Magic Fountain of Montjuïc:

- Location: Plaça de Carles Buïgas, 1, 08038 Barcelona
- Overview: The Magic Fountain is a large, illuminated fountain located in front of the National Art Museum of Catalonia, offering nightly music and light shows.
- Highlights: The stunning fountain displays set to music and the magnificent backdrop of Montjuïc Hill.

7. Palau de la Música Catalana:
- Location: Carrer del Palau de la Música, 4-6, 08003 Barcelona
- Overview: The Palau de la Música Catalana is a modernist concert hall known for its intricate stained glass and decorative features.
- Highlights: The spectacular stained glass ceiling, the ornate concert hall, and the elegant mosaics.

8. Montserrat:

- Location: Monistrol de Montserrat, 08199 Barcelona
- Overview: Montserrat is a mountain range near Barcelona known for its unique rock formations and the Montserrat Monastery, which houses the famous Black Madonna.
- Highlights: The basilica, the stunning views from the summit, and hiking trails leading to various hermitages.

9. Barcelona Beaches:
- Locations: Barcelona has several urban beaches along its coast, including Barceloneta Beach, Bogatell Beach, and Nova Icaria Beach.
- Overview: These sandy beaches offer opportunities for relaxation, swimming, sunbathing, and water sports.

10. Camp Nou:

- Location: Carrer d'Aristides Maillol, 12, 08028 Barcelona

- Overview: Camp Nou is the home stadium of FC Barcelona, offering stadium tours and a museum that celebrates the club's history and achievements.

- Highlights: The Camp Nou Experience tour, which includes the changing rooms, player's tunnel, and the trophy room.

11. Park de la Ciutadella:
   - Location: Passeig de Picasso, 21, 08003 Barcelona
   - Overview: This urban park is an oasis in the city, featuring a boating lake, sculptures, gardens, and cultural attractions.
   - Highlights: The Cascada fountain, the boating lake, and the peaceful Umbracle greenhouse.

12. Montjuïc:

- Location: Montjuïc Hill, southwest of the city center
- Overview: Montjuïc is a hill with numerous attractions, including Montjuïc Castle, the Magic Fountain, and cultural venues.
- Highlights: The history and panoramic views from Montjuïc Castle, the Magic Fountain light shows, and the Joan Miró Foundation.

13. Picasso Museum:
- Location: Carrer Montcada, 15-23, 08003 Barcelona
- Overview: The Picasso Museum houses one of the most extensive collections of artworks by the 20th-century Spanish artist Pablo Picasso.
- Highlights: The collection of Picasso's early works, his artistic evolution, and the museum's historic setting.

14. Tibidabo:

- Location: Plaça del Tibidabo, 08035 Barcelona
- Overview: Tibidabo Mountain features an amusement park with vintage rides and offers panoramic views of the city from its summit.
- Highlights: The roller coasters, the Tibidabo Church, and the panoramic observation area.

15. Barcelona Aquarium:
- Location: Moll d'Espanya del Port Vell, s/n, 08039 Barcelona
- Overview: The Barcelona Aquarium is a family-friendly attraction featuring thousands of marine species, including sharks and rays.
- Highlights: The Oceanarium, the underwater tunnel, and interactive exhibits for children.

16. Hospital de Sant Pau:

- Location: Carrer de Sant Antoni Maria Claret, 167, 08025 Barcelona
- Overview: A UNESCO World Heritage Site, this modernist hospital complex is a masterpiece of architect Lluís Domènech i Montaner.
- Highlights: The stunning mosaics, colorful pavilions, and serene gardens.

17. Poble Espanyol:
- Location: Av. Francesc Ferrer i Guàrdia, 13, 08038 Barcelona
- Overview: Poble Espanyol is an open-air architectural museum showcasing the diversity of Spanish architectural styles.
- Highlights: Replicas of Spain's most iconic buildings, craft workshops, and themed squares.

18. CosmoCaixa Barcelona:

- Location: Carrer d'Isaac Newton, 26, 08022 Barcelona
- Overview: CosmoCaixa is a science museum with interactive exhibits, a planetarium, and a tropical rainforest exhibit.
- Highlights: The Amazon Rainforest exhibit, the Geological Wall, and the immersive planetarium shows.

19. Barcelona Zoo:
- Location: Parc de la Ciutadella, s/n, 08003 Barcelona
- Overview: Barcelona Zoo is home to a wide variety of animals, including mammals, birds, reptiles, and marine life.
- Highlights: The dolphin show, the primate house, and the rare white lions.

20. Barcelona Botanical Garden:

- Location: Carrer del Doctor Font i Quer, 2, 08038 Barcelona
- Overview: This tranquil botanical garden features a diverse collection of plants and showcases Mediterranean and world flora.
- Highlights: The cactus and succulent garden, the tropical greenhouse, and themed gardens.

Each of these attractions offers a unique experience, from the architectural wonders of Gaudí to the natural beauty of Montserrat and the cultural richness of museums and historical sites. Barcelona's diverse array of attractions ensures there's something to captivate every visitor.

- Beaches (Barceloneta)
Barcelona's Beaches: Barceloneta and Beyond

Barcelona is renowned for its beautiful urban beaches, and Barceloneta Beach is one of the most iconic and popular among them. However, the city offers several other fantastic beaches along its coastline. Let's explore these sandy stretches along with their highlights:

1. Barceloneta Beach:

- Location: Passeig Marítim de la Barceloneta, 08003 Barcelona
- Overview: Barceloneta Beach is the closest and most famous beach to the city center, making it easily accessible for both locals and tourists.
- Highlights: Golden sands, lively atmosphere, numerous beachfront bars and restaurants (chiringuitos), water sports, and iconic W Barcelona Hotel.

2. Bogatell Beach:

- Location: Passeig Marítim de la Mar Bella, 08005 Barcelona
- Overview: Bogatell Beach is known for its cleanliness and family-friendly environment. It's a bit further from the city center than Barceloneta, offering a more relaxed atmosphere.
- Highlights: Beach volleyball courts, ping pong tables, jogging paths, and a variety of water sports facilities.

3. Nova Icaria Beach:

- Location: Carrer de la Marina, 08005 Barcelona
- Overview: Nova Icaria Beach is close to the Port Olímpic area and offers a blend of relaxation and recreation.
- Highlights: Beachfront restaurants, water sports, beachside bars, and the Port Olímpic marina with its lively nightlife.

4. Mar Bella Beach:

- Location: Passeig Marítim de la Mar Bella, 08005 Barcelona
- Overview: Mar Bella Beach is known for its open-minded atmosphere and is often considered the city's "gay beach."
- Highlights: LGBTQ+ friendly environment, beach volleyball courts, windsurfing opportunities, and a designated nudist area.

5. Ocata Beach:

- Location: Carrer de l'Atlàntida, 08302 El Masnou, Barcelona (located outside the city, accessible by train)
- Overview: Ocata Beach is situated in the town of El Masnou, just a short train ride from Barcelona, and offers a quieter, more suburban beach experience.
- Highlights: Tranquility, clean sands, water sports, beachside restaurants, and a charming seaside town.

Barcelona's beaches offer something for everyone, whether you're looking for a lively beach with a vibrant atmosphere, a quieter and more relaxed setting, or a family-friendly environment. Each beach has its unique character, but they all share the backdrop of the Mediterranean Sea and the warm Catalan sun, making them perfect places to unwind and enjoy the coastal beauty of the city.

6. Cultural Experiences

Museums (e.g., Picasso Museum, Joan Miró Foundation)
Llet's explore these museums in Barcelona in more detail:

1. Museu Picasso (Picasso Museum):

- Location: Carrer Montcada, 15-23, 08003 Barcelona
- Overview: The Picasso Museum is a must-visit for art enthusiasts. It boasts one of the most extensive collections of artworks by the 20th-century Spanish artist Pablo Picasso. The museum is housed in five adjoining medieval palaces, creating a unique and historic backdrop for Picasso's works. The collection spans his early years and artistic evolution.

2. Museu Nacional d'Art de Catalunya (MNAC):
- Location: Palau Nacional, Parc de Montjuïc, 08038 Barcelona
- Overview: MNAC is a treasure trove of Catalan art, with collections that span from the Romanesque period

to the modern era. The museum is located in the stunning National Palace on Montjuïc Hill and offers panoramic views of the city. Visitors can admire masterpieces by renowned artists and explore Catalan history through art.

3. Museu d'Història de Barcelona (MUHBA):

- Location: Various sites throughout Barcelona, including the Gothic Quarter
- Overview: MUHBA is a network of museums and archaeological sites that delve into the rich history of Barcelona. The exhibitions include Roman ruins, medieval buildings, and artifacts that tell the story of the city's evolution. Highlights include the Barcelona City History Museum in Plaça del Rei and the Temple of Augustus.

4. CosmoCaixa Barcelona:
- Location: Carrer d'Isaac Newton, 26, 08022 Barcelona

- Overview: CosmoCaixa is a captivating science museum known for its interactive exhibits, planetarium, and a tropical rainforest exhibit. It's an engaging destination for families and science enthusiasts, where you can explore various aspects of the natural world and scientific phenomena.

5. Museu Frederic Marès:

- Location: Plaça de Sant Iu, 5, 08002 Barcelona
- Overview: This charming museum is set in a historic building and showcases the eclectic collection of sculptor Frederic Marès. The museum features an array of art and artifacts, from sculptures and religious relics to everyday objects, offering insights into the artist's life and interests.

6. Museu Marítim de Barcelona (Maritime Museum):
- Location: Av. de les Drassanes, s/n, 08001 Barcelona
- Overview: Housed in the historic Royal Shipyards, this museum is a journey through Barcelona's maritime history. Visitors can explore an array of historical ships,

including the impressive Royal Galley of Don John of Austria, as well as artifacts related to navigation and maritime culture.

7. Museu Blau (Natural Science Museum of Barcelona):

   - Location: Plaça de Leonardo da Vinci, 4-5, 08019 Barcelona
   - Overview: Museu Blau is a natural history museum that offers engaging exhibitions on paleontology, geology, and the diversity of life on Earth. It's an excellent destination for those interested in the natural world and the history of our planet.

8. Centre de Cultura Contemporània de Barcelona (CCCB):
   - Location: Carrer de Montalegre, 5, 08001 Barcelona
   - Overview: CCCB is a hub for contemporary culture and art. It hosts a diverse range of exhibitions, performances, talks, and events that explore contemporary issues, making it a dynamic and thought-provoking cultural space.

9. Museu de la Música (Music Museum):

- Location: L'Auditori, Carrer de Lepant, 150, 08013 Barcelona
- Overview: The Music Museum, situated within the Auditori building, offers a fascinating journey into the world of music. Visitors can explore an extensive collection of musical instruments from different eras and cultures and gain insights into the history of music.

10. Museu Egipci de Barcelona (Egyptian Museum):
- Location: Carrer Valencia, 284, 08007 Barcelona
- Overview: This museum is a captivating tribute to Egyptian culture and history. It houses an impressive collection of artifacts, including mummies, sculptures, and other treasures from ancient Egypt. Visitors can embark on a journey through the mysteries of this ancient civilization.

11. Museu del Disseny de Barcelona (Design Museum):

- Location: Plaça de les Glòries Catalanes, 37-38, 08018 Barcelona
- Overview: The Design Museum explores the world of design, featuring objects related to fashion, graphics, and product design. The museum showcases the evolution of design and its impact on our daily lives.

12. CaixaForum Barcelona:
- Location: Av. de Francesc Ferrer i Guàrdia, 6-8, 08038 Barcelona
- Overview: CaixaForum is an arts and cultural center that hosts a diverse range of exhibitions, concerts, and events. It offers a platform for contemporary art, culture, and creativity, making it a vibrant and ever-changing cultural space.

13. Museu de la Moto (Motorcycle Museum):

- Location: Carrer de la Mar, 92, 08980 Sant Feliu de Llobregat, Barcelona (located outside the city)
- Overview: For motorcycle enthusiasts, this museum offers a captivating journey through the history of motorcycles. The collection includes a wide range of historic and iconic motorcycle models, showcasing their evolution and the art of motorcycle design.

15. Museu de la Colònia Güell:

- Location: Carrer Claudi Güell, 6, 08690 Santa Coloma de Cervelló, Barcelona (located outside the city)
- Overview: This museum is located in the Güell Colony, a worker's community designed by architect Antoni Gaudí. The museum focuses on the industrial and architectural heritage of the colony, including the famous crypt designed by Gaudí. Visitors can learn about the social and cultural aspects of this unique experiment in early 20th-century urban planning.

16. Museu de Cera de Barcelona (Wax Museum):
   - Location: Passatge de la Banca, 7, 08002 Barcelona
   - Overview: The Wax Museum in Barcelona features lifelike wax figures of historical and famous personalities from various eras. It offers a unique and interactive way to learn about historical and contemporary figures, including celebrities, scientists, and world leaders.

17. Museu del Ferrocarril (Railway Museum):

- Location: Plaça Eduard Maristany, s/n, 08800 Vilanova i la Geltrú, Barcelona (located outside the city)
- Overview: Situated in the historic train station of Vilanova i la Geltrú, this museum showcases the history of rail transportation in Catalonia. Visitors can explore a fascinating collection of locomotives, carriages, and other railway artifacts, as well as learn about the development of railways in the region.

18. Museu de la Moto (Motorcycle Museum):
- Location: Carrer de la Mar, 92, 08980 Sant Feliu de Llobregat, Barcelona (located outside the city)
- Overview: For motorcycle enthusiasts, this museum offers a captivating journey through the history of motorcycles. The collection includes a wide range of historic and iconic motorcycle models, showcasing their evolution and the art of motorcycle design.

19. Museu de la Ciència (Science Museum):

- Location: Parc de la Ciutadella, 08003 Barcelona
- Overview: This museum, situated in Parc de la Ciutadella, offers an engaging and interactive experience for visitors of all ages. It explores various aspects of science, from physics and astronomy to biology and technology. The museum features hands-on exhibits, educational displays, and an exciting planetarium.

Barcelona's museums offer a delightful mix of history, art, culture, science, and technology. Whether you're passionate about renowned artists like Picasso, curious about the ancient civilizations of Egypt, or eager to explore the frontiers of science, Barcelona's museums provide a wealth of knowledge and an immersive journey into various aspects of human creativity and discovery. Don't miss the opportunity to explore the vibrant cultural tapestry of this fascinating city.

- Flamenco shows

Let's explore the top flamenco venues in Barcelona in more detail:

1. Palacio del Flamenco:

- Location: Carrer de Balmes, 139, 08008 Barcelona
- Overview: Palacio del Flamenco is an elegant venue located in the Eixample district. It offers daily flamenco performances that showcase the raw emotion and vibrant rhythms of this art form. The venue's setting exudes a Spanish atmosphere, and you can enjoy traditional Spanish cuisine while being immersed in the passionate world of flamenco. The show features talented dancers, singers, and guitarists who bring the stage to life with their powerful performances.

2. Tablao Cordobes:

- Location: La Rambla, 35, 08002 Barcelona
- Overview: Tablao Cordobes is one of the most renowned flamenco venues in Barcelona. It's located right on La Rambla, making it easily accessible. The venue hosts high-quality flamenco performances with exceptional dancers, singers, and musicians. Guests can choose from various dinner options to enhance their evening while enjoying the captivating show. Tablao Cordobes offers an authentic and memorable flamenco experience in a historical setting.

3. Los Tarantos:

- Location: Plaça Reial, 17, 08002 Barcelona
- Overview: Los Tarantos is an iconic flamenco venue situated in the heart of the Gothic Quarter. It's one of Barcelona's oldest and most legendary tablaos, known for its intimate atmosphere and traditional performances. Here, you can witness the essence of flamenco in a cozy setting. The venue hosts nightly shows with both established artists and emerging talents, making each evening unique and captivating.

4. El Tablao de Carmen:

- Location: Poble Espanyol, Av. de Francesc Ferrer i Guàrdia, 13, 08038 Barcelona

- Overview: El Tablao de Carmen pays tribute to the legendary dancer Carmen Amaya and offers a unique experience in the Poble Espanyol. The setting resembles a Spanish village, providing a cultural and historical context for the show. The performances here are a blend of traditional and contemporary flamenco, capturing the heart and soul of this passionate art form. Diners can enjoy Spanish cuisine while being transported into the world of Carmen Amaya.

5. Palau Dalmases:

- Location: Carrer de Montcada, 20, 08003 Barcelona
- Overview: Palau Dalmases is located in a historic palace in the El Born district. The venue provides an enchanting backdrop for nightly flamenco performances. With its elegant setting, including beautiful courtyards, this location offers an intimate and artistic experience. The shows at Palau Dalmases feature exceptional artists who express the depth of flamenco through dance, music, and song.

6. Tarantos Club:

- Location: Plaça Reial, 17, 08002 Barcelona
- Overview: Tarantos Club is another long-standing and respected flamenco venue situated in Plaça Reial. With a rich history, this venue continues to offer nightly shows featuring passionate and skilled flamenco artists. The intimate setting allows guests to get up close and personal with the artists, experiencing the intensity and emotion of this captivating art form.

7. Flamenco Barcelona:

- Locations: Various venues in Barcelona
- Overview: Flamenco Barcelona is a company that organizes flamenco shows at various venues throughout the city. You can check their schedule to find performances during your visit. They offer a diverse range of experiences and styles, making it a great option to explore different facets of flamenco in Barcelona.

These venues collectively represent the heart and soul of
Barcelona's vibrant flamenco scene. Whether you're a
long-time admirer of this passionate art form or a
newcomer looking to be enchanted by the power of
dance, music, and emotion, Barcelona's flamenco shows
provide an unforgettable and culturally rich experience.
Enjoy the magic of flamenco in this dynamic city.

   - Festivals and events

Let's explore these festivals and events in Barcelona in
more detail:

1. La Mercè:

   - Date: Late September
   - Overview: La Mercè is Barcelona's grandest annual
festival, honoring the city's patron saint, the Virgin of
Mercy. The celebration lasts several days and is a vibrant
showcase of Catalan traditions and modern creativity.
The streets come alive with parades, concerts, street

theater, and other cultural events. A major highlight is the "correfoc," a fire run featuring costumed demons and fireworks, and the captivating castells, human tower displays. It's a time when Barcelona bursts with life and creativity, allowing you to immerse yourself in the heart of Catalan culture.

2. Primavera Sound:
   - Date: Late May or early June
   - Overview: Primavera Sound is one of Barcelona's most iconic music festivals, renowned for its diverse and cutting-edge lineup. The festival offers a platform for both emerging and established artists across various music genres. From indie rock to electronic and pop, Primavera Sound creates a dynamic and inclusive music experience at the Parc del Fòrum and Parc de la Pau. It's a must-visit for music enthusiasts seeking to discover new sounds and enjoy the performances of renowned bands.

3. Sonar Festival:

- Date: June
- Overview: Sonar Festival is a globally recognized electronic music festival that combines music, arts, and technology. It's held in various venues across Barcelona, offering both daytime and nighttime experiences. The festival boasts a lineup of top DJs and live electronic acts, and it's known for its art installations and multimedia presentations. Sonar provides an immersive journey into the world of electronic music and digital arts, making it a magnet for music and tech enthusiasts.

4. Barcelona International Jazz Festival:
- Date: October to December
- Overview: The Barcelona International Jazz Festival is a well-established event that caters to jazz lovers. It brings together an array of jazz styles and artists, both classic and contemporary, at various venues across the city. The festival offers an opportunity to appreciate the improvisational and soulful nature of jazz in intimate

and atmospheric settings, including the historic Palau de la Música Catalana.

5. Grec Festival:

- Date: July
- Overview: The Grec Festival is Barcelona's summer arts festival, and it takes its name from the Greek-style amphitheater on Montjuïc where many performances are held. The festival features a diverse program, including theater, dance, music, and other cultural events. It's a chance to enjoy open-air performances under the starry Barcelona sky, and the festival has a history of bringing both local and international talent to the stage, creating a rich cultural tapestry.

6. Carnaval de Barcelona:

- Date: February or March
- Overview: Barcelona's Carnival is a joyful celebration featuring colorful parades, costumes, and lively street parties. While not as extensive as the Carnival in some other Spanish cities, Barcelona's celebration is unique and local. It's a time when the streets are filled with laughter, music, and dancing, providing a vibrant and inclusive atmosphere for both residents and visitors.

7. Festes de Gràcia:

- Date: August
- Overview: Festes de Gràcia is a neighborhood festival celebrated in the Gràcia district, known for its imaginative street decorations. Each year, the residents of Gràcia compete to transform their streets into intricate and colorful works of art, creating a charming and artistic atmosphere. The festival also features live music, cultural activities, and traditional Catalan festivities.

8. Festes de Sants:
  - Date: August
  - Overview: Similar to Festes de Gràcia, Festes de Sants is a neighborhood festival, taking place in the Sants district of Barcelona. It involves street decorations, music, and cultural events. The residents of Sants express their creativity by decorating the streets with a mix of imaginative and traditional themes.

9. Diada de Sant Jordi:

  - Date: April 23rd
  - Overview: Diada de Sant Jordi, also known as Saint George's Day, is a unique Catalan tradition celebrated by exchanging books and roses. The streets are adorned with bookstalls, authors signing their works, and flower stands. It's a celebration of literature, culture, and love, where people express their affection for one another through these symbolic gifts.

10. Pride Barcelona:
   - Date: Late June
   - Overview: Pride Barcelona is a joyful and inclusive LGBTQ+ Pride festival that promotes diversity and equality. The event features colorful parades, parties, cultural activities, and talks on LGBTQ+ issues. It's a time for the LGBTQ+ community and allies to come together and celebrate love and acceptance.

11. Fira de Santa Llúcia:

   - Date: Early December
   - Overview: Fira de Santa Llúcia is a traditional Christmas market held in front of the Barcelona Cathedral. Here, you can discover a wide variety of seasonal decorations, gifts, and traditional Catalan nativity scenes. It's a festive and heartwarming place to experience the holiday spirit and find unique Christmas items.

12. Sant Joan:
   - Date: Night of June 23rd
   - Overview: Sant Joan is a lively and energetic celebration that takes place on the night of the summer solstice. People gather on Barcelona's beaches to light bonfires, set off fireworks, and enjoy beach parties. It's a night of music, dancing, and merriment as the city welcomes the arrival of summer.

13. Guitar BCN:

   - Date: Various dates throughout the year
   - Overview: Guitar BCN is an annual music festival that celebrates the versatility of the guitar. The festival showcases a wide range of guitar-related genres, from classical and flamenco to rock and blues, featuring performances by renowned guitarists and emerging talents.

14. Festival Internacional de Jazz de Barcelona:
   - Date: Various dates throughout the year
   - Overview: The Festival Internacional de Jazz de Barcelona is internationally acclaimed and features a diverse program of jazz styles and artists. It provides a platform for both legendary and contemporary jazz musicians, bringing the magic of jazz to the city throughout the year.

15. Easter Week (Semana Santa):

   - Date: Typically falls in March or April
   - Overview: While Barcelona's Easter Week celebrations may not be as elaborate as in some other Spanish cities, the city still observes this important religious event. Processions, religious events, and cultural activities take place during this period, providing an opportunity to experience the rich traditions of Semana Santa.

16. Maremagnum Free Music Concerts:

- Date: Various dates throughout the year
- Overview: The Maremagnum shopping center in Port Vell hosts free open-air concerts that feature a variety of musical genres, from rock and pop to electronic and world music. These events provide an opportunity to enjoy live music in a scenic waterfront setting.

17. Sala Montjuïc:

- Date: Summer months
- Overview: Sala Montjuïc is an open-air cinema event held at

the Montjuïc Castle. It offers screenings of classic and contemporary films in a unique setting. It's a chance to enjoy movies under the stars with the Barcelona skyline as a backdrop.

18. Summer Nights at La Pedrera:
- Date: Summer months

- Overview: La Pedrera, designed by architect Antoni Gaudí, hosts summer evening concerts on its iconic rooftop. Visitors can enjoy live music and stunning views of the city, making it a magical experience for both music and architecture enthusiasts.

19. The Chocolate Museum Workshops:
   - Date: Throughout the year
   - Overview: The Chocolate Museum in Barcelona offers workshops and tastings that allow you to delve into the world of chocolate making. You can learn about the history, production, and art of chocolate, all while indulging your sweet tooth.

20. International Beer Festival:

   - Date: Various dates
   - Overview: Barcelona hosts an International Beer Festival, featuring craft beers from around the world. It's an excellent opportunity to explore a wide range of beer styles, from traditional ales to innovative craft brews.

21. Maremàgnum Open Air Concerts:
   - Date: Various dates
   - Overview: The Maremàgnum shopping center in Port Vell offers a series of free open-air concerts featuring diverse musical genres, providing entertainment for a wide range of tastes.

22. Festival Internacional de Jazz de Barcelona:

   - Date: Various dates throughout the year
   - Overview: This internationally acclaimed jazz festival brings together a diverse lineup of jazz artists, spanning from legendary musicians to contemporary talents. The festival offers a captivating journey through the world of jazz, with performances held in various venues across Barcelona.

23. Barcelona Film Festival (BCN Film Fest):
   - Date: Spring
   - Overview: BCN Film Fest is a cinematic event that celebrates both international and Spanish films. It features film screenings, premieres, and discussions

with directors and actors, offering a unique opportunity to engage with the world of cinema.

24. World Press Photo Exhibition:
   - Date: Various dates
   - Overview: The World Press Photo Exhibition is an annual showcase of award-winning photojournalism. It's hosted at the CCCB (Centre de Cultura Contemporània de Barcelona), allowing visitors to explore compelling and impactful photographic stories from around the world.

25. Santa Eulalia Festival:

   - Date: February
   - Overview: The Santa Eulalia Festival is a winter celebration in honor of Barcelona's co-patron saint. It features parades, cultural events, and festivities that offer a unique perspective on Catalan traditions.

26. Barcelona Boat Show:

- Date: October
- Overview: The Barcelona Boat Show is a significant nautical event held at Port Vell. It's a platform for showcasing boats, water sports, marine technology, and the latest trends in the world of boating.

27. Tapa a Tapa Barcelona:

- Date: Various editions throughout the year
- Overview: Tapa a Tapa Barcelona is a culinary event that invites you to explore the city's gastronomic scene. Participating restaurants offer a selection of tapas, allowing you to savor a wide range of flavors and styles.

28. OFFF Barcelona:
- Date: April
- Overview: OFFF Barcelona is a creative conference and festival that brings together digital and design

professionals. It features talks, workshops, and presentations on design, innovation, and digital art.

29. Salon del Cómic de Barcelona:

- Date: Spring
- Overview: The Salon del Cómic de Barcelona is a comic book and graphic novel convention that draws fans, artists, and publishers. Visitors can meet artists, discover new works, and participate in cosplay, making it a haven for comic enthusiasts.

30. Sant Cugat Fantastic Film Festival:

- Date: October
- Overview: While not in Barcelona itself, the Sant Cugat Fantastic Film Festival is worth mentioning. It's a film festival specializing in science fiction, fantasy, and horror movies, offering a unique cinematic experience in the nearby town of Sant Cugat.

Barcelona's rich event calendar ensures there's always something exciting happening, catering to a wide range of interests and passions. Whether you're captivated by music, arts, cuisine, or cultural traditions, the city offers a multitude of opportunities to engage with its vibrant and dynamic spirit throughout the year.

7. Food and Dining

- Local cuisine and specialties

Let's explore the local cuisine and specialties of Barcelona and Catalonia in more detail:

1. Paella:

- Overview: Although paella is originally from Valencia, it's widely enjoyed in Barcelona and along the Catalan coast. The most common variation is seafood paella, featuring a saffron-infused rice cooked with a medley of seafood like shrimp, mussels, squid, and often a variety of local fish.

2. Fideuà:

- Overview: Fideuà is sometimes referred to as "paella's cousin" because it shares a similar cooking method but uses short, thin noodles instead of rice. Seafood fideuà is a beloved variant, showcasing the flavors of the Mediterranean.

3. Crema Catalana:

- Overview: Crema Catalana is a luscious dessert akin to crème brûlée but with a Catalan twist. The custard base is infused with cinnamon and lemon zest, lending it a unique flavor. The crispy caramelized sugar topping adds a delightful contrast in texture.

4. Esqueixada:

- Overview: Esqueixada is a vibrant Catalan salad made with salt cod, tomatoes, onions, bell peppers, olives, and a tangy vinaigrette. The dish is both refreshing and appetizing, perfect for a warm day.

5. Escalivada:
- Overview: Escalivada is a straightforward yet flavorful dish of grilled and marinated vegetables, often including eggplants, red peppers, and onions. The vegetables are typically drizzled with olive oil and garlic, creating a delightful side dish or tapa.

6. Botifarra:
- Overview: Botifarra is a type of Catalan sausage, usually made from pork and seasoned with garlic and other spices. It's often enjoyed grilled or served with white beans, creating a delicious and hearty meal.

7. Calcots:
- Overview: Calcots are similar to spring onions and are a quintessential Catalan treat. They are grilled over open flames and served with a special romesco sauce during calcotadas, a social and gastronomic event that marks the onset of spring.

8. Butifarra Amb Mongetes:
- Overview: A classic Catalan dish that combines grilled butifarra sausages with mongetes (white beans) and a flavorsome garlic sauce. The sausages are typically seasoned with pepper and garlic, making for a mouthwatering combination.

9. Coca:

   - Overview: Coca is a versatile flatbread or pastry that comes in various forms, both savory and sweet. It's commonly topped with ingredients like vegetables, fruits, or small pieces of meat. It's often enjoyed as a snack or light meal.

10. Bacalao a la Llauna:

   - Overview: Bacalao a la Llauna is a dish featuring codfish that's typically baked in a clay dish with tomatoes, garlic, and olive oil. The result is a tender and flavorful fish dish, and it's often served with crusty bread to soak up the delicious sauce.

11. Suquet de Peix:

   - Overview: Suquet de Peix is a rich seafood stew, particularly popular in coastal areas. The dish includes a variety of fish and seafood, simmered in a broth that's infused with garlic, paprika, and saffron. It's a comforting and hearty dish, often served with crusty bread to mop up the flavorful sauce.

12. Gambes a la Plancha:

   - Overview: Gambes a la Plancha are prawns grilled to perfection and seasoned simply with salt and olive oil. The key to this dish's success is the freshness of the prawns, allowing their natural flavors to shine.

13. Trinxat:

- Overview: Trinxat is a hearty dish made from mashed potatoes, cabbage, and pork. It's often pan-fried until crispy and served with a fried egg on top, creating a satisfying and flavorful meal, especially during the colder months.

14. Xató:
   - Overview: Xató is a Catalan salad that combines endive and other vegetables. What sets it apart is the rich and flavorful sauce, typically made from almonds, hazelnuts, garlic, and peppers. It's a harmonious blend of textures and tastes.

15. Pan con Tomate:
   - Overview: Pan con Tomate is a simple yet beloved Catalan staple. It consists of bread that's rubbed with ripe tomatoes, garlic, and olive oil, often sprinkled with a pinch of salt. It's a classic accompaniment to many Catalan dishes.

16. Catalan Cream:
   - Overview: Catalan Cream, also known as "crema Catalana," is a delightful dessert that bears similarities to crème brûlée. The custard base is flavored with cinnamon and lemon zest, creating a subtly

citrusy and spiced profile. It's often topped with caramelized sugar for a contrasting crunchy layer.

17. Espresso Coffee with a Twist:

- Overview: Coffee culture is strong in Barcelona, and you'll often be served a simple yet flavorful espresso. It's common to pair your espresso with a twist, such as a slice of lemon peel or a bit of sugar, allowing you to personalize your coffee experience.

18. Catalan Wines:
   - Overview: Catalonia is renowned for its wine production. Explore local wine varieties, such as Priorat, known for its bold reds; Penedès, famous for its whites and Cavas (sparkling wines); and Terra Alta, which produces a wide range of wines.

19. Catalan Cheeses:
   - Overview: Catalonia offers a diverse selection of cheeses. Mató is a fresh, creamy cheese often paired with honey and walnuts. Garrotxa is a semi-hard goat cheese with a mild, earthy flavor. Formatge de l'Alt Urgell is a cow's milk cheese with blue veins, delivering a bold and distinct taste.

20. Panellets:
   - Overview: Panellets are small, round sweets made from marzipan. They are traditionally enjoyed during All Saints' Day (La Castanyada) in Catalonia. These delightful treats come in various flavors and are often rolled in pine nuts, providing a unique texture and nutty taste.

Exploring Barcelona's local cuisine and specialties is a culinary journey that lets you savor the authentic flavors of Catalonia. Whether you're indulging in fresh seafood, hearty stews, or delightful desserts, the local gastronomy captures the essence of the region's rich food culture, making every meal a memorable experience.

- Best restaurants and tapas bars
Let's explore these exceptional restaurants and tapas bars in Barcelona in more detail:

Best Restaurants in Barcelona:

1. Tickets:

- Overview: Tickets is a culinary masterpiece created by the Adrià brothers, who are renowned for their groundbreaking work at elBulli, once considered the world's best restaurant. This whimsical tapas restaurant offers avant-garde creations that blend art and gastronomy. The dining experience is both playful and extraordinary, with a menu that constantly evolves and surprises.

2. Disfrutar:
   - Overview: Disfrutar is a Michelin-starred restaurant that embodies innovation and creativity. The chefs draw on traditional Catalan flavors but present them in a modern and imaginative way. The tasting menu is a culinary adventure, showcasing unique dishes that engage the senses.

3. Els Pescadors:

   - Overview: Situated in the picturesque Barceloneta neighborhood, Els Pescadors is a seafood lover's paradise. This restaurant offers the freshest Mediterranean seafood prepared with simplicity and elegance. The menu includes classics like paella and grilled fish, all served in a charming coastal setting.

4. Cinc Sentits:
   - Overview: Cinc Sentits is a Michelin-starred restaurant that takes the concept of dining to another level. The name translates to "Five Senses," and the

restaurant focuses on creating an immersive experience for diners. Their tasting menu showcases Catalan and Mediterranean cuisine with a contemporary twist.

5. Can Culleretes:

   - Overview: Can Culleretes holds the distinction of being one of the oldest restaurants in Barcelona, dating back to 1786. It's a historic establishment that serves traditional Catalan dishes. The menu includes staples like escalivada, suquet de peix, and rabbit with prunes.

6. Quimet & Quimet:
   - Overview: Quimet & Quimet is a beloved family-run tapas bar famous for its montaditos, small open sandwiches piled high with a variety of gourmet ingredients. The bar is tiny and often crowded, but the atmosphere is lively, and the flavors are exceptional.

7. Pakta:

  - Overview: Pakta is part of the Michelin-starred Grupo 5 restaurant family, and it's a culinary adventure that fuses Japanese and Peruvian cuisines. The tasting menu is a mesmerizing journey through flavors and textures, and it's served in a stylish and contemporary setting.

8. Lasarte:
  - Overview: Lasarte is one of Barcelona's culinary gems, boasting three Michelin stars. Helmed by Chef Martín Berasategui, the restaurant offers an extraordinary fine dining experience. The tasting menu features dishes that are not only visually stunning but also perfectly crafted, utilizing the finest ingredients.

9. Dos Palillos:

- Overview: Dos Palillos is another Michelin-starred gem in Barcelona, known for its fusion of Asian and Spanish flavors. The concept revolves around sharing plates and tapas, and the menu showcases innovative and delectable combinations.

10. Can Majó:

- Overview: Can Majó is an authentic seafood restaurant nestled in the Barceloneta neighborhood. With its delightful paellas, fresh grilled fish, and paella with lobster, it offers a genuine taste of Mediterranean cuisine. The seaside location makes it a perfect spot for a leisurely lunch or dinner.

Best Tapas Bars in Barcelona:

1. Bar del Pla:

   - Overview: Bar del Pla is a cozy tapas bar in the El Born district, known for its welcoming atmosphere and delectable tapas. The menu offers a range of traditional and creative dishes, allowing you to explore a variety of flavors and textures.

2. El Xampanyet:
   - Overview: El Xampanyet is a legendary tapas bar located in the El Born district. It's celebrated for its sparkling wine (Cava) and classic Spanish tapas. The bar exudes a warm and lively ambiance, and it's a fantastic place to enjoy traditional favorites.

3. Bormuth:

- Overview: Bormuth is a stylish and modern tapas bar situated in the Gothic Quarter. Here, you'll find a diverse array of traditional and innovative tapas. The menu incorporates quality ingredients and creative presentations, making it a must-visit for tapas enthusiasts.

4. Cervecería Catalana:
   - Overview: Cervecería Catalana is a bustling and popular tapas bar that offers an extensive selection of small plates and a vibrant atmosphere. It's an excellent spot to experience the energy of Barcelona's tapas scene while savoring a wide range of culinary delights.

5. La Cova Fumada:

- Overview: La Cova Fumada is an unassuming gem located in Barceloneta, known for its traditional Catalan dishes. The bomba, a type of potato croquette, is a standout dish at this historic establishment. The small size and intimate feel add to its charm.

6. Vinitus:

- Overview: Vinitus is a trendy and contemporary tapas bar with a focus on seafood, grilled dishes, and inventive tapas. The restaurant offers a vibrant atmosphere and an extensive menu, providing a delightful dining experience.

7. Bar Pinotxo:
- Overview: Bar Pinotxo is a renowned counter located in the bustling Mercat de Sant Josep de la Boqueria, also known as La Boqueria Market. The bar is celebrated for its classic Catalan dishes, hearty breakfasts, and traditional tapas. The charming market setting adds to the authenticity of the experience.

8. La Boqueria:

- Overview: La Boqueria Market is an iconic food market in Barcelona. It houses numerous stalls and counters that offer a wide variety of fresh and cooked foods, including tapas. You can explore a myriad of culinary offerings, from seafood and charcuterie to traditional and creative tapas.

9. La Pepita:

  - Overview: La Pepita is a hip and modern tapas bar located in the Gràcia neighborhood. It's known for its inventive and flavorful tapas, particularly its "pepitas," which are open-faced sandwiches packed with delectable ingredients. The menu often includes innovative combinations that delight the palate.

10. Els Quatre Gats:

  - Overview: Els Quatre Gats is a historic modernist café and tapas bar, famous for its association with renowned artists like Pablo Picasso. It combines culture, cuisine, and art, making it a unique destination. The menu offers a blend of traditional and contemporary Catalan dishes, and it's an excellent place to enjoy a meal in a historical setting.

When exploring Barcelona's culinary scene, whether you're seeking inventive and Michelin-starred dining or traditional and authentic tapas, you'll find a wealth of options to satisfy your culinary cravings. The city's diverse and vibrant food culture promises a delightful and memorable dining experience at every turn.

- Food markets (e.g., La Boqueria)
Let's delve into the diverse and vibrant food markets of Barcelona, each with its own unique charm and offerings:

1. Mercat de Sant Josep de la Boqueria (La Boqueria):

- Overview: La Boqueria is perhaps the most famous food market in Barcelona and is located just off the bustling La Rambla. It's a sensory wonderland where you'll find a kaleidoscope of colors, aromas, and flavors. The market offers an extensive range of fresh produce, including fruits, vegetables, meats, and seafood. It's a great place to sample local specialties, such as jamón ibérico, fresh fruit juices, and various Catalan dishes. There are also stands selling spices, chocolates, and other gourmet products.

2. Mercat de Sant Antoni:

- Overview: Mercat de Sant Antoni is known for its fresh produce, meats, and seafood. What makes it unique is the Sunday market outside the building, where you can find second-hand book stalls that cater to collectors and book enthusiasts. The market has undergone a recent renovation, with the opening of an underground supermarket in addition to the traditional market.

3. Mercat de Santa Caterina:

- Overview: This market, located in the Ribera district, is not only renowned for its high-quality fresh produce but also for its striking, undulating modernist architecture. It's a hub for locals who appreciate the diverse array of fresh foods, including fruits, vegetables, meats, and seafood. Inside, you'll also find a contemporary restaurant that serves Catalan and Mediterranean dishes.

4. Mercat de la Concepció:
  - Overview: Situated in the Eixample district, Mercat de la Concepció is a lively market known for its fresh produce, flowers, and plants. It's an excellent place to shop for local ingredients and enjoy the vibrant atmosphere. The market often hosts events and activities, making it a hub for the community.

5. Mercat de la Llibertat:

  - Overview: Located in the Gràcia neighborhood, Mercat de la Llibertat is celebrated for its fresh produce, meats, and seafood. This market places a strong emphasis on local and organic products, making it a favorite among those who value sustainability and quality.

6. Mercat de Sant Gervasi:
  - Overview: Found in the Sant Gervasi neighborhood, this market is recognized for its high-quality produce

and artisanal products. It attracts locals who seek premium ingredients and is a testament to the appreciation of fine foods in Barcelona.

7. Mercat de Galvany:

- Overview: Mercat de Galvany is another gem in the Sant Gervasi district, known for its elegant modernist architecture. It offers a delightful range of fresh produce, meats, and gourmet foods. The market retains a sense of history and sophistication.

8. Mercat de Sarrià:
- Overview: Nestled in the Sarrià neighborhood, Mercat de Sarrià is a beloved market among locals. It provides fresh foods, including fruits, vegetables, meats, and seafood. The market offers an authentic glimpse into neighborhood life and culinary traditions.

9. Mercat del Ninot:

- Overview: Situated in the Eixample district, Mercat del Ninot is a modern market offering a diverse selection of fresh products. It's particularly known for its seafood and meats. The market's contemporary design adds a touch of sophistication to the shopping experience.

10. Mercat de Sants:
- Overview: Mercat de Sants is known for its quality fresh produce, seafood, and meats. It's a place that thrives on community life, offering locals a reliable source of ingredients while creating a warm and inviting atmosphere.

11. Mercat de Hostafrancs:

- Overview: Located near Sants train station, Mercat de Hostafrancs serves as a convenient shopping destination for both locals and travelers. The market features a variety of stalls selling fresh food products, from fruits and vegetables to meats and seafood.

12. Mercat de la Sagrada Família:

- Overview: Mercat de la Sagrada Família is strategically positioned near the iconic Sagrada Família basilica. Here, you can explore a variety of fresh foods and local specialties after visiting the famous landmark. The market allows you to immerse yourself in the neighborhood's daily life while indulging in a diverse range of ingredients and culinary experiences.

Barcelona's food markets are not just places to shop for groceries; they're cultural hubs where locals and visitors can connect with the region's culinary heritage. Each market reflects the character and traditions of its neighborhood, making them fantastic places to explore the heart and soul of the city's food culture.

8. Shopping

- Popular shopping districts

Let's explore the distinctive shopping districts in Barcelona, each offering a unique blend of styles and experiences:

1. Passeig de Gràcia:

- Overview: Passeig de Gràcia is Barcelona's most upscale shopping avenue, known for its luxury boutiques and high-end fashion stores. This iconic street is lined with impressive modernist buildings, some designed by the renowned architect Antoni Gaudí. It's home to international fashion brands like Chanel, Gucci, Prada, and Louis Vuitton, as well as Spanish designers and jewelry shops. The avenue is a paradise for fashion enthusiasts and architecture lovers alike.

2. La Rambla:

- Overview: La Rambla is one of the most famous streets in Barcelona and is a bustling hub for tourists and shoppers. While it's celebrated for its street performers, outdoor markets, and lively atmosphere, you can also find a variety of shops along the promenade. There are souvenir shops selling everything from trinkets to traditional Spanish fans and crafts. It's a convenient location to pick up mementos of your visit.

3. Gothic Quarter (Barri Gòtic):

   - Overview: The Gothic Quarter is the historic heart of Barcelona, and it's a captivating place to explore boutique shops, art galleries, and artisan stores. Wandering through its labyrinth of narrow streets and squares, you'll stumble upon vintage clothing shops, unique jewelry boutiques, and local craft stores. It's also home to the awe-inspiring Catedral de Barcelona.

4. El Raval:
   - Overview: El Raval is a diverse neighborhood known for its multicultural vibe and artsy atmosphere. It's a

great place to discover trendy and vintage shops, making it ideal for those seeking unique fashion finds. The neighborhood also boasts a vibrant nightlife scene and numerous dining options.

5. El Born:

  - Overview: El Born is another district offering a mix of designer boutiques and independent shops, particularly around the Passeig del Born. Here, you can explore fashion, art, and jewelry stores while immersing yourself in the medieval charm of the area. The district is also home to the striking Santa Maria del Mar church.

6. Gràcia:
  - Overview: The Gràcia district has a bohemian and artsy vibe, making it a treasure trove of independent boutiques, vintage shops, and artisan craft stores. Plaça del Sol is a popular spot for shopping, dining, and soaking in the neighborhood's artistic spirit. The district

is known for its vibrant festivals, like the Festa Major de Gràcia.

7. Poble Espanyol:

  - Overview: Poble Espanyol is an architectural museum complex that replicates various styles of Spanish architecture. It also includes a shopping village where you can purchase Spanish artisan products, crafts, and regional specialties from different parts of Spain. It's a fantastic place to discover the rich cultural diversity of the country in one location.

8. Diagonal Mar:
  - Overview: Diagonal Mar, near the sea, is a shopping and entertainment center with a selection of fashion stores, electronics shops, and restaurants. It's a popular

destination for both shopping and leisure, offering a pleasant coastal setting.

9. Maremagnum:

- Overview: Situated by the waterfront, Maremagnum is a shopping and entertainment center with a variety of fashion, accessory, and gift shops. It's an excellent spot to spend an afternoon near the sea. The mall also boasts a cinema, restaurants, and bars.

10. L'Illa Diagonal:
- Overview: L'Illa Diagonal is a modern shopping center featuring a mix of international and local brands. It offers a variety of fashion, home goods, and gourmet food stores. You can explore a wide range of shopping options in a contemporary and convenient setting.

11. Glòries:

- Overview: Glòries is situated near the Torre Glòries (formerly known as the Agbar Tower) and is a multifaceted shopping and dining complex. The mall encompasses a range of stores, from clothing to electronics, and is often a convenient shopping destination for those in the area.

12. Sant Antoni Market:
    - Overview: Sant Antoni Market recently underwent a significant renovation, making it a hub not only for fresh produce but also for its Sunday market. This market features stalls with antiques, books, and collectibles, attracting both locals and visitors.

13. Port Vell:

- Overview: The area around Port Vell, near the marina, includes various shops such as fashion boutiques, jewelry stores, and nautical equipment outlets. It's a charming place to shop, dine, and enjoy views of the harbor.

14. Poble Sec:

- Overview: Poble Sec is a lesser-known neighborhood with a growing number of boutique shops and creative spaces. It's ideal for those who seek to discover hidden gems and explore an emerging arts and shopping scene.

These shopping districts in Barcelona cater to a diverse range of tastes and preferences, from high-end luxury shopping to quirky vintage finds and artisan crafts. Whether you're seeking fashion, art, antiques, or local specialties, Barcelona's shopping scene offers something unique and exciting for every type of shopper.

- Souvenirs and local products
Let's delve into the world of Barcelona's souvenirs and local products, each capturing the essence of this vibrant city:

1. Spanish Ceramics:
   - Overview: Barcelona's rich tradition of ceramics is reflected in its colorful and intricately designed pottery. You can find everything from hand-painted tiles and plates to decorative figurines and vases. These ceramics often feature traditional motifs and patterns that are emblematic of Spanish and Catalan culture.

2. Sangria Sets:
   - Overview: A sangria set is a wonderful way to bring a taste of Spain back home with you. These sets usually include a beautifully crafted ceramic pitcher and matching glasses. They are ideal for serving the famous Spanish drink, sangria, and are both practical and decorative souvenirs.

3. Gaudí Souvenirs:

 - Overview: Antoni Gaudí's architectural influence is omnipresent in Barcelona. You can find a wide array of souvenirs inspired by his iconic works, including the Sagrada Família, Park Güell, and Casa Batlló. These items range from miniature architectural models and sculptures to prints, postcards, and even Gaudí-themed jewelry.

4. Spanish Fans:

 - Overview: Spanish hand fans are elegant and practical souvenirs. Typically made of wood and adorned with vibrant designs, these fans are a symbol of Spanish culture. They come in various styles, from traditional to contemporary, and can be both decorative and functional.

5. Espadrilles:

 - Overview: Traditional Spanish espadrilles are comfortable and stylish footwear made from natural materials like jute and canvas. They are especially popular during the summer months and are available in a variety of colors and designs. Espadrilles are a fashionable and wearable souvenir.

6. Iberian Ham:

 - Overview: Spain is celebrated for its world-class Iberian ham, particularly jamón ibérico. You can purchase this delicious and highly sought-after ham as a souvenir. It's available in various forms, from whole legs to vacuum-sealed packs, making it a tasty and distinctive gift.

7. Olive Oil:
   - Overview: Spain is one of the top olive oil producers in the world, and Barcelona offers an excellent selection of olive oils. Look for bottles of extra virgin olive oil or sets that include an array of flavored oils, allowing you to savor the diverse and delightful flavors of Spain.

8. Wine and Cava:
   - Overview: Catalonia, the region surrounding Barcelona, is home to some outstanding wineries and vineyards. Consider bringing back a bottle of Catalan wine or Cava, a Spanish sparkling wine similar to Champagne. These make for excellent gifts and a way to savor the flavors of the region.

9. Chocolate:
   - Overview: Barcelona boasts some fantastic chocolate shops, offering a wide range of high-quality chocolate bars, truffles, and other delectable treats. Look for unique and locally crafted chocolates in various flavors and styles to take home or share with loved ones.

10. Turron:
   - Overview: Turron is a traditional Spanish nougat, often made with almonds and honey. You can find a variety of turron in Barcelona, and it's a delightful and sweet souvenir to bring back. It's perfect for enjoying a taste of Spain's confectionery tradition.

11. Spanish Leather Goods:
  - Overview: Spain is renowned for its quality leather products. Barcelona offers an excellent selection of leather handbags, wallets, belts, and shoes. These items are stylish, durable, and make for practical and fashionable souvenirs.

12. Flamenco Accessories:
  - Overview: Flamenco is an integral part of Spanish culture, and you can find souvenirs related to this art form. Consider castanets, shawls, and flamenco-style fans as distinctive reminders of your time in Spain.

13. Spanish Tiles:
  - Overview: Barcelona is famous for its decorative tiles, often featuring intricate and colorful designs. You can find ceramic or porcelain tiles that depict traditional Spanish patterns or elements from Gaudí's architectural works. These tiles are perfect for home decor or as wall art.

14. Castells Figurines:
  - Overview: Castells are human towers, a traditional Catalan spectacle. You can find small figurines that depict these tower formations. These unique souvenirs represent an important aspect of Catalan culture and are both charming and symbolic.

15. Catalan Wine Glasses:

- Overview: Barcelona is near some of Catalonia's excellent wine regions. Consider purchasing Catalan wine glasses to enjoy your Spanish wine in style. These glasses are often elegant and come in various designs.

16. Local Art and Prints:
   - Overview: Barcelona is a thriving hub for artists and galleries. Explore local art shops to discover unique artworks, prints, and posters that capture the essence of the city. Whether you're into contemporary art or traditional styles, there's something for every art enthusiast.

17. Paella Pans:
   - Overview: If you've fallen in love with Spanish cuisine, consider bringing back a paella pan. These are available in various sizes and are ideal for recreating the iconic Spanish dish, paella, at home. It's a practical and culinary souvenir.

18. Gourmet Foods:
   - Overview: Barcelona's local markets and specialty shops are filled with gourmet foods. Look for items like saffron, spices, and preserved goods such as roasted peppers and artichoke hearts. These ingredients will allow you to recreate Spanish flavors in your own kitchen.

19. Handcrafted Jewelry:
   - Overview: Barcelona is home to numerous talented jewelry artisans. Look for handcrafted jewelry items,

including pieces made from silver and gemstones. These items are both beautiful and meaningful as souvenirs.

20. Spanish Tableware:
   - Overview: Spanish tableware, including colorful plates, bowls, and glasses, often features vibrant designs and patterns. You can bring a touch of Mediterranean flair to your dining table by selecting pieces that capture the essence of Spanish cuisine and hospitality.

21. Castanets:
   - Overview: Castanets are traditional Spanish percussion instruments used in flamenco and other Spanish dances. They come in various sizes and designs, making them a unique and musical souvenir from your visit to Barcelona.

22. Spanish Guitar:
   - Overview: Barcelona is a city deeply connected to the world of music, and a Spanish guitar can be a fantastic and melodious souvenir. Look for quality instruments in specialized music stores to take home a piece of Spain's musical heritage.

23. Regional Herbs and Spices:
   - Overview: Barcelona's markets offer an array of regional herbs and spices. Select ingredients like saffron, pimentón (smoked paprika), and local dried herbs to infuse your culinary creations with Spanish flavors and aromas.

24. Paella Ingredients:
   - Overview: If you're a fan of paella, consider gathering the ingredients needed to recreate this iconic Spanish dish at home. Look for bags of paella rice, saffron, and the essential seafood or meats to create an authentic paella feast.

25. Spanish Cookbooks:
   - Overview: Barcelona's bookstores and markets offer an assortment of Spanish cookbooks, allowing you to explore and recreate the diverse flavors of Spanish cuisine. Choose from a wide selection of recipe books that cater to various culinary interests and skill levels.

26. Artisanal Soaps and Perfumes:
   - Overview: Barcelona has a growing artisanal soap and perfume industry. Look for handmade soaps, fragrant candles, and natural perfumes crafted with local scents and botanicals, providing you with a sensory memento of your visit.

27. Traditional Hats and Headwear:
   - Overview: Spain is known for its distinctive hats and headwear, from the Andalusian-style wide-brimmed hats to Basque berets. These hats are not only stylish but also evoke the spirit of Spanish culture.

28. T-shirts and Apparel:
   - Overview: You'll find a variety of T-shirts and apparel featuring Barcelona and Catalonia-themed designs.

From street markets to boutiques, there are options for those looking to sport their Barcelona pride.

29. Castanuelas (Castanets):
   - Overview: Castanuelas are traditional Spanish percussion instruments often used in flamenco dancing. These hand instruments come in various sizes and styles, and you can choose a pair as a unique and musical souvenir.

30. Soccer Memorabilia:
   - Overview: FC Barcelona, one of the world's most famous soccer clubs, has a significant presence in the city. Soccer fans can explore official club stores for jerseys, scarves, and other memorabilia to commemorate their visit.

31. Bespoke Tailoring:
   - Overview: Barcelona is known for its fashion and tailoring. For a truly unique souvenir, consider having a piece of clothing tailored to fit you perfectly, reflecting your personal style.

32. Local Craft Beer and Vermouth:
   - Overview: Barcelona has seen a rise in craft beer and vermouth production. Look for local brands and breweries offering unique and flavorful options that you can take home or enjoy during your stay.

33. Unique Bags and Accessories:

- Overview: Barcelona's fashion scene is diverse and innovative. Discover boutiques and shops selling one-of-a-kind bags, belts, and accessories crafted by local designers, allowing you to take home a piece of Barcelona's fashion culture.

34. Spanish Language Books:
   - Overview: If you're interested in learning Spanish or simply want to immerse yourself in the language, you can purchase Spanish language books, novels, or dictionaries to continue your linguistic journey beyond your visit.

35. Gourmet Chocolates:
   - Overview: Apart from traditional chocolates, Barcelona has artisanal chocolatiers creating delightful gourmet chocolates with innovative flavors and designs. These chocolates make for indulgent and unique souvenirs.

36. Local Crafts and Artisanal Goods:
   - Overview: Barcelona's artisanal crafts are diverse, including handwoven textiles, pottery, and woodwork. Explore local markets and craft fairs to find one-of-a-kind handmade items created by skilled artisans.

37. Lladro Porcelain:
   - Overview: Lladro is a world-famous Spanish porcelain company known for its elegant figurines. Barcelona offers numerous stores where you can find

these exquisite pieces, each crafted with precision and artistry.

38. Spanish Fashion Brands:
   - Overview: Barcelona boasts a vibrant fashion scene, and you can explore the collections of local Spanish designers. Look for clothing, shoes, and accessories from both established and emerging brands.

39. Local Artisanal Beer:
   - Overview: The craft beer scene has been on the rise in Barcelona. Consider taking home bottles of local artisanal beer, showcasing the city's creativity and flavors.

40. Handcrafted Jewelry:
   - Overview: Barcelona's artisan jewelers create unique and exquisite pieces. Explore jewelry boutiques for handcrafted items made from precious metals and gemstones, providing you with a personalized and timeless keepsake.

These souvenirs and local products embody the spirit of Barcelona and offer a diverse range of options for travelers to choose from. Whether you're an art enthusiast, a culinary explorer, or a fashion connoisseur, Barcelona has something special to suit your tastes and provide lasting memories of your visit to this remarkable city.

9. Nightlife

- Bars and clubs

Bars
Barcelona's nightlife is as diverse as it is vibrant, with an
array of bars to suit all tastes and preferences. Let's take
an in-depth look at some of the popular types of bars
and the venues within them:

1. El Born Barrio:
   - Overview: El Born is a historic neighborhood with
narrow streets and a charming atmosphere, making it an
excellent place to start your night out. Its bars are
known for their unique character and atmosphere.
   - Recommendations: Bar Marsella is a legendary
absinthe bar with a vintage ambiance, frequented by
famous artists and writers in the past. El Xampanyet is
renowned for its sparkling wine (cava) and delicious
tapas.

2. Gothic Quarter (Barri Gòtic):
   - Overview: The Gothic Quarter is a labyrinth of
narrow streets and historic buildings, making it a
captivating location for bar-hopping. You'll find bars
hidden away in centuries-old buildings and intimate
courtyards.
   - Recommendations: Bar del Pi, located next to the
beautiful Santa Maria del Pi church, is known for its
cozy atmosphere and serves a wide range of drinks.

Ocaña is a trendy cocktail bar with an artistic and stylish vibe.

3. Poble Sec:
   - Overview: Poble Sec is an emerging nightlife district with a variety of bars, tapas places, and pintxos bars. It's a lively neighborhood known for its artistic and alternative scene.
   - Recommendations: Bar Seco offers a relaxed setting, ideal for starting your evening with cocktails and craft beers. Carrer de Blai is a street known for its pintxos bars, making it a great spot to experience this Basque-style cuisine.

4. Raval:
   - Overview: The Raval neighborhood offers a diverse selection of bars and is known for its multicultural and artsy atmosphere. You can find bars for all tastes, from classic to trendy.
   - Recommendations: Joaquin Costa is a cozy and welcoming bar known for its creative cocktails. Marsella, dating back to the 19th century, is a historical absinthe bar with a unique atmosphere.

5. Gràcia:
   - Overview: Gràcia is a bohemian neighborhood with a lively nightlife. You'll find numerous bars and terraces, making it a great place to explore and enjoy a relaxed evening.
   - Recommendations: La Rovira is a popular spot for craft beer enthusiasts, offering a wide selection of beers.

Plaça del Sol is a lively square with various bars and restaurants, perfect for enjoying a vibrant atmosphere.

6. Passeig del Born:
   - Overview: Passeig del Born in El Born is lined with bars and cafes, making it an attractive destination for a night out. It's an area with a mix of traditional and trendy bars.
   - Recommendations: Miramelindo is known for its innovative cocktails and lively atmosphere. Bar Lobo offers a trendy setting for cocktails and tapas.

7. Eixample:
   - Overview: Eixample is known for its wide boulevards and elegant atmosphere. This district offers numerous bars that cater to a quieter and more upscale night out.
   - Recommendations: Dry Martini is an iconic cocktail bar known for its classic drinks and refined setting. Marmalade Bar offers a blend of cocktails and lounges in an elegant atmosphere.

8. Beaches and Beach Clubs:
   - Overview: Barcelona's beaches offer a unique nightlife experience. Beachfront bars and clubs are perfect for enjoying drinks with the Mediterranean sea as your backdrop.
   - Recommendations: Shoko Barcelona, Opium Barcelona, and CDLC (Carpe Diem Lounge Club) are popular beachfront venues offering music, dancing, and drinks by the sea.

9. Rooftop Bars:
   - Overview: Barcelona's skyline is dotted with rooftop bars offering panoramic views of the city. These venues provide an upscale and luxurious nightlife experience.
   - Recommendations: Eclipse Barcelona, The Serras Rooftop, and La Isabela at Hotel 1898 are some of the city's best rooftop bars, providing stunning views and upscale settings for a memorable night out.

10. Cocktail Bars:
   - Overview: Barcelona has an emerging cocktail culture, with bars known for their innovative and classic cocktails. These venues offer a more sophisticated nightlife experience.
   - Recommendations: Paradiso Bar is a hidden gem behind a pastrami bar, offering unique and inventive cocktails. Dry Martini, an iconic cocktail bar, serves classic drinks with precision and style.

11. Irish Pubs:
   - Overview: For those seeking a taste of Ireland in Barcelona, there are several Irish pubs where you can enjoy a pint of Guinness, live music, and a friendly atmosphere.
   - Recommendations: Flaherty's Irish Pub is a popular choice with a traditional Irish pub atmosphere, complete with live sports screenings. Kitty O'Shea's is known for its welcoming ambiance and hearty pub food.

12. Craft Beer Bars:

- Overview: Barcelona has seen a surge in the craft beer scene, with many bars and taprooms offering a wide selection of craft beers. Craft beer enthusiasts will find plenty to explore.
- Recommendations: Black Lab Brewhouse is a well-regarded brewpub known for its craft beer creations. Garage Beer Co. is a local taproom with a dynamic range of craft beer options.

13. Jazz Bars:
- Overview: Barcelona boasts a thriving jazz scene with bars that host live jazz performances in intimate and welcoming settings.
- Recommendations: Jamboree is an iconic jazz club that has hosted renowned musicians. Robadors 23 offers a cozy atmosphere and live jazz performances.

14. Gay Bars:
- Overview: Barcelona's Eixample district is the heart of the city's LGBTQ+ scene, featuring a variety of gay bars and clubs.
- Recommendations: Punto BCN is a popular gay bar with a lively atmosphere, drag shows, and regular events. The Black Bull is a long-standing gay bar known for its friendly environment and great cocktails.

15. Tropical Bars:
- Overview: Tropical bars bring a taste of the Caribbean to Barcelona with exotic cocktails and laid-back atmospheres.

- Recommendations: Rumpus Room is a stylish and trendy tropical bar offering a range of unique cocktails. Tiki Bar Barcelona transports you to a tiki paradise with its island-inspired drinks and decor.

16. Tapas Bars:
  - Overview: Many tapas bars in Barcelona offer a taste of Spanish cuisine along with your drinks, making for a complete and delicious night out.
  - Recommendations: El Xampanyet is a famous spot for traditional Spanish tapas, particularly paired with sparkling wine. Quimet & Quimet is celebrated for its creative tapas and extensive wine selection.

17. Electro and Dance Clubs:
  - Overview: If dancing the night away is your goal, Barcelona has a thriving club scene, featuring world-renowned DJs and electronic music.
  - Recommendations: Razzmatazz is a legendary nightclub with multiple rooms, each offering different music genres. Pacha Barcelona and Sutton Club are popular electro and dance clubs known for hosting top DJs.

18. Alternative and Indie Bars:
  - Overview: Barcelona's alternative music scene is vibrant, with bars that offer live music and an indie atmosphere.
  - Recommendations: Sidecar Factory Club is a long-established bar known for its indie and alternative

music nights. Heliogàbal is an intimate venue that hosts live music and various artistic events.

Barcelona's nightlife is a rich tapestry of experiences, reflecting the city's diverse culture and spirit. Whether you're in the mood for a cozy night out with traditional Spanish tapas, dancing until dawn in a trendy club, or sipping cocktails with panoramic views, Barcelona offers an eclectic array of bars to make your night unforgettable. So, take your pick and explore the city's dynamic nightlife scene.

Clubs.
Barcelona's club scene is vibrant and diverse, offering a wide range of venues that cater to different tastes and atmospheres. Here's an in-depth look at some of the popular clubs in Barcelona:

1. Razzmatazz:

- Overview: Razzmatazz is an iconic and sprawling club in Barcelona. It's renowned for its versatility, featuring five different rooms, each with a unique music style, from indie and pop to electronic and techno. The club has hosted famous DJs and live acts, making it a must-visit for music enthusiasts.

- Atmosphere: Razzmatazz offers an energetic and dynamic atmosphere, drawing a diverse crowd of locals and tourists.

2. Pacha Barcelona:

- Overview: Part of the internationally recognized Pacha brand, Pacha Barcelona is synonymous with luxury and glamour. It's known for hosting top DJs, especially in the electronic and house music genres. The club boasts an elegant and stylish setting.

- Atmosphere: Pacha Barcelona offers a high-end and upscale atmosphere, attracting a fashionable and well-dressed crowd.

3. Sutton Club:

- Overview: Sutton Club is a sophisticated and stylish venue, considered one of Barcelona's most exclusive nightspots. It hosts a mix of music styles, including commercial hits and electronic beats, and offers an opulent setting.

- Atmosphere: Sutton Club is known for its glamorous and upscale atmosphere, drawing a trendy and fashionable clientele.

4. Opium Barcelona:

- Overview: Opium Barcelona is a beachfront club, combining stunning views with an electric atmosphere. It offers a fusion of music styles, from commercial hits to electronic beats, making it a versatile destination for partygoers.

- Atmosphere: Opium Barcelona provides a sleek and modern atmosphere, popular among a diverse crowd of locals and tourists.

5. CDLC (Carpe Diem Lounge Club):

- Overview: CDLC is a beach club and lounge, making it an ideal location to enjoy cocktails, music, and beach views. It's a stylish venue located on the beachfront, creating a unique nightlife experience.

- Atmosphere: CDLC offers a luxurious and fashionable beach club atmosphere, attracting those who appreciate seaside indulgence.

6. Shoko Barcelona:

- Overview: Situated beachside, Shoko Barcelona is a club known for its fusion of music styles, including hip-hop, R&B, and electronic beats. The club's contemporary design and beachfront location make it a favored choice for night owls.

- Atmosphere: Shoko Barcelona provides a stylish and modern atmosphere, popular among those who enjoy both music and beach vibes.

7. Eclipse Barcelona:

- Overview: Eclipse Barcelona is a rooftop bar and club located on the 26th floor of the W Barcelona hotel. It offers panoramic views of the city and the Mediterranean. The venue hosts a variety of events, making it a destination for a luxurious night out.

- Atmosphere: Eclipse Barcelona offers an upscale and sophisticated rooftop atmosphere, attracting those seeking a lavish experience with breathtaking city views.

8. Macarena Club:

- Overview: Macarena Club is known for its focus on underground electronic music. It's a smaller and more intimate club, creating an alternative and inclusive nightlife environment.

- Atmosphere: Macarena Club offers an underground and intimate atmosphere, perfect for electronic music enthusiasts and a more dedicated crowd.

9. Catwalk Club:

- Overview: Catwalk Club is located in the Gothic Quarter, offering a diverse lineup of music styles. It's a popular venue among both locals and tourists, making it a great place to experience Barcelona's nightlife.
- Atmosphere: Catwalk Club provides a lively and welcoming atmosphere, drawing partygoers of various backgrounds.

10. Sala Apolo:
- Overview: Sala Apolo is a renowned club that caters to multiple music styles, including indie, electronic, and pop. The club hosts live concerts in addition to DJ sessions, ensuring a varied and engaging nightlife experience.
- Atmosphere: Sala Apolo offers a dynamic and diverse atmosphere, making it a favorite among music

enthusiasts looking for live performances and club nights.

11. Shoko Beach Club:

- Overview: Shoko Beach Club is an extension of Shoko Barcelona, offering daytime beach parties and evening club events. Located on the beachfront, it provides a lively atmosphere, making it an ideal place to enjoy the best of both worlds: beach relaxation and clubbing.
- Atmosphere: Shoko Beach Club offers a dynamic and energetic atmosphere, blending the beach scene with club vibes.

12. R33:
- Overview: R33 is a club situated near Las Ramblas, known for its electronic music and underground scene. It's a smaller venue with a dedicated crowd of electronic music enthusiasts.
- Atmosphere: R33 provides an intimate and immersive atmosphere for those who appreciate underground electronic beats.

13. The Sutton Social:

- Overview: The Sutton Social is an elegant space within the Sutton Club complex. It offers a more relaxed and chillout atmosphere compared to the main club area, making it a great place to start your night or wind down.
- Atmosphere: The Sutton Social provides a more laid-back and refined atmosphere, allowing guests to enjoy a sophisticated and relaxed ambiance.

14. Sala BeCool:
- Overview: Sala BeCool is a club known for its diverse music programming, spanning from indie to techno. It

caters to a broad spectrum of music enthusiasts and offers a platform for emerging and established artists.

- Atmosphere: Sala BeCool creates a vibrant and eclectic atmosphere, making it a place for those looking for diverse and alternative music experiences.

15. Egg Barcelona:

- Overview: Located in the Eixample district, Egg Barcelona specializes in electronic music. It's a prime destination for techno and house music aficionados, featuring both local and international DJs.

- Atmosphere: Egg Barcelona offers an immersive atmosphere for electronic music lovers, creating a space where they can dance the night away.

16. Macarena Beach Club:

- Overview: Macarena Beach Club offers a more relaxed beachfront atmosphere compared to Macarena

Club. It's a great spot for daytime relaxation and enjoying the Mediterranean beach scene.

- Atmosphere: Macarena Beach Club provides a laid-back and beachy atmosphere, making it an ideal choice for those seeking daytime beach vibes.

17. Catwalk Club:

- Overview: Catwalk Club, located in the Gothic Quarter, offers a dynamic lineup of music styles, making it a popular choice among locals and tourists. It's a welcoming and inclusive venue.

- Atmosphere: Catwalk Club offers a lively and vibrant atmosphere, making it a favored spot for those who want to experience the diversity of Barcelona's nightlife.

18. Nitsa Club:

- Overview: Nitsa Club is situated within Sala Apolo, dedicated to electronic music. It has a rich history and has hosted renowned DJs and producers, making it a must-visit for fans of electronic beats.

- Atmosphere: Nitsa Club provides an electric and immersive atmosphere for electronic music enthusiasts, delivering an unforgettable clubbing experience.

Barcelona's club scene is known for its diversity, ensuring that you can find a club that matches your musical tastes and mood. From beachfront parties to underground beats, stylish luxury venues to intimate and immersive spaces, the city offers an array of choices to enjoy the vibrant nightlife and create memorable nights out in Barcelona.

- Nightlife districts

Barcelona's nightlife districts each offer a unique and vibrant atmosphere, catering to different tastes and preferences. Here's a detailed look at the key nightlife districts in Barcelona:

1. Gothic Quarter (Barri Gòtic):
- Overview: The Gothic Quarter is the heart of Barcelona's historic center, known for its winding narrow streets, centuries-old architecture, and charming medieval atmosphere. Its vibrant nightlife is centered around lively plazas and hidden corners, where you can find a mix of bars, clubs, and live music venues.
- Atmosphere: The Gothic Quarter exudes an enchanting and historic ambiance, creating a magical setting for a night out. It's perfect for those who appreciate history and an intimate, atmospheric setting.

2. El Born:

- Overview: El Born, situated adjacent to the Gothic Quarter, is a lively and artistic neighborhood. It offers a vibrant nightlife scene with a concentration of bars, tapas places, and clubs, especially along Passeig del Born.

- Atmosphere: El Born combines historic charm with an energetic and artistic vibe, attracting a diverse crowd looking for a lively night out.

3. Poble Sec:

- Overview: Poble Sec is an up-and-coming neighborhood with a growing reputation for nightlife. Carrer de Blai is a highlight, known for its pintxos (small snacks) bars. It offers a more local and alternative nightlife experience.

- Atmosphere: Poble Sec provides a dynamic and local atmosphere, making it a great choice for those looking for authentic and unpretentious nightlife.

4. Raval:

- Overview: The Raval neighborhood is diverse and multicultural, creating an eclectic nightlife scene. It features a wide range of bars and clubs, from cocktail bars to historic establishments.

- Atmosphere: Raval offers a multicultural and dynamic atmosphere, drawing an array of people seeking everything from craft cocktails to traditional Spanish experiences.

5. Gràcia:
  - Overview: Gràcia is known for its bohemian atmosphere and offers an abundance of bars, terraces, and live music venues. The Plaça del Sol is a popular spot with a variety of bars.
  - Atmosphere: Gràcia provides a laid-back and vibrant neighborhood atmosphere, making it a wonderful choice for a relaxed and community-oriented night out.

6. Eixample:
  - Overview: Eixample is a district with wide boulevards and a more upscale ambiance. In the Eixample Esquerra area, you can find numerous cocktail bars and lounges, making it ideal for a quieter night out.
  - Atmosphere: Eixample offers an elegant and stylish atmosphere, perfect for those who appreciate classic cocktails and a more sophisticated evening.

7. Poblenou:
  - Overview: Poblenou, in the northeastern part of the city, is known for its creative and alternative scene. It's home to numerous beachfront bars and clubs, offering a unique blend of urban and seaside vibes.
  - Atmosphere: Poblenou provides a creative and laid-back atmosphere, making it a favorite among the artistic and alternative crowd.

8. Port Olímpic:
  - Overview: Located by the beach, Port Olímpic offers a variety of beach clubs, bars, and lounges. It's a prime

destination for beachfront nightlife, with many venues hosting DJs and live music.

- Atmosphere: Port Olímpic offers a relaxed and beachy atmosphere, combining music and drinks with a beautiful view of the Mediterranean.

9. Barceloneta:

- Overview: Barceloneta, another beachfront neighborhood, is famous for its chiringuitos (beach bars) and beach clubs. It's a hub of beachfront nightlife, especially during the summer months.

- Atmosphere: Barceloneta provides a lively and summery beach atmosphere, attracting those looking for beach parties and seafront cocktails.

10. Sant Gervasi-Galvany:

- Overview: Located in the upper part of the city, Sant Gervasi-Galvany offers a more laid-back and refined nightlife scene. It focuses on cocktail bars, lounges, and elegant venues.

- Atmosphere: Sant Gervasi-Galvany offers a relaxed and upscale atmosphere, making it an ideal choice for a more mature and sophisticated night out.

Each of these nightlife districts in Barcelona has its unique charm and appeal, catering to a wide range of tastes and preferences. Whether you're looking for historic charm, beachfront fun, artistic vibes, or upscale elegance, you'll find a neighborhood that matches your idea of a memorable night out in this dynamic and diverse city.

10. Day Trips

Here's an in-depth look at each of the recommended day trip destinations from Barcelona:

1. Montserrat:
   - Overview: Montserrat is a stunning mountain range located about an hour's train ride from Barcelona. The highlight is the Montserrat Monastery, home to the revered Black Madonna statue. The unique rock formations and hiking trails make it a popular pilgrimage site and a great destination for nature lovers.

2. Sitges:
   - Overview: Sitges, often referred to as the "St. Tropez of Spain," is a charming coastal town located just 30 minutes by train from Barcelona. Known for its beautiful beaches, vibrant nightlife, and artistic culture, it's a great destination for a relaxed day by the sea.

3. Tarragona:
   - Overview: Tarragona, an hour from Barcelona by train, is a city with a rich Roman heritage. Explore well-preserved Roman ruins, including an amphitheater and aqueduct, in addition to its charming old town.

4. Girona:

   - Overview: About an hour from Barcelona, Girona is a picturesque city with a beautifully preserved medieval old town. Highlights include the Girona Cathedral, the colorful houses along the Onyar River, and the historic Jewish Quarter.

5. Costa Brava:
   - Overview: The Costa Brava, located within a few hours from Barcelona, is known for its stunning coastline and picturesque beaches. Visit charming coastal towns like Calella de Palafrugell, Tossa de Mar, and Cadaqués for a taste of Mediterranean beauty.

6. Figueres:
   - Overview: Figueres is famous for the Dalí Theatre-Museum, a surrealistic masterpiece created by artist Salvador Dalí. The museum is an eclectic and imaginative journey into the mind of the renowned painter.

7. Cadaqués:
   - Overview: Cadaqués is a picturesque seaside village near Figueres. It's famous for its crystal-clear waters, beautiful beaches, and its association with Salvador Dalí, who had a house in the area.

8. Penedès Wine Region:
   - Overview: Located within an hour's drive from Barcelona, the Penedès region is known for its vineyards and cava production. Take a winery tour to explore the wine-making process and enjoy tastings of cava, a sparkling wine produced in Catalonia.

9. Vic:

   - Overview: Vic, located less than an hour by train from Barcelona, boasts a charming old quarter with narrow streets, a bustling market, and the stunning Vic

Cathedral. It's a great place to immerse yourself in Catalan culture.

10. Montseny Natural Park:
   - Overview: Montseny, located about an hour's drive from Barcelona, is a protected natural park with lush forests, hiking trails, and diverse wildlife. It's an excellent destination for nature enthusiasts and hikers.

11. Cardona:
   - Overview: Cardona is a historic town featuring an impressive medieval castle known for housing a unique salt mountain. Explore the historic castle, visit the salt mines, and enjoy panoramic views of the surroundings.

12. Cistercian Route:

   - Overview: The Cistercian Route takes you to three stunning Cistercian monasteries in Catalonia: Poblet, Santes Creus, and Vallbona de les Monges. These monasteries are known for their architectural beauty and peaceful surroundings.

13. Sant Sadurni d'Anoia:
   - Overview: Sant Sadurni d'Anoia is at the heart of Catalonia's cava (sparkling wine) production region. Take a tour of cava cellars, learn about the wine-making process, and enjoy tastings in this charming town.

14. Catalan Pyrenees:

   - Overview: The Catalan Pyrenees, located within a few hours of Barcelona, offer breathtaking natural beauty and outdoor activities. Whether you're into hiking, skiing, or simply enjoying mountain scenery, this region has it all.

These day trips from Barcelona provide a wealth of experiences, from cultural exploration and historic discoveries to enjoying natural beauty and outdoor adventures. You can tailor your day trips to your interests and make the most of your time exploring the diverse surroundings of Catalonia.

15. Cadaqués:

  - Overview: Cadaqués, a coastal gem near Figueres, is a picturesque seaside village famous for its crystal-clear waters, beautiful beaches, and its strong connection to Salvador Dalí, who had a house in the area. Explore the charming town, its coastal promenade, and the Dalí House-Museum.

16. Penedès Wine Region:

  - Overview: The Penedès wine region, located within an hour's drive from Barcelona, is known for its vineyards and cava production. Visit wineries and cellars, learn about the wine-making process, and savor tastings of cava, a sparkling wine produced in Catalonia. It's a delightful day trip for wine connoisseurs and enthusiasts.

17. Montseny Natural Park:

- Overview: Montseny Natural Park is situated about an hour's drive from Barcelona. It's a protected area characterized by lush forests, hiking trails, and diverse wildlife. Nature enthusiasts can explore the park's biodiversity and enjoy outdoor activities like hiking and birdwatching.

18. Cardona:
- Overview: Cardona is a historic town known for its impressive medieval castle, Cardona Castle, which houses a unique salt mountain that's one of the largest in Europe. Explore the historic castle, visit the salt mines, and enjoy panoramic views of the surroundings.

19. Cistercian Route:
- Overview: The Cistercian Route takes you to three remarkable Cistercian monasteries in Catalonia: Poblet, Santes Creus, and Vallbona de les Monges. These monasteries are celebrated for their architectural

beauty, serene surroundings, and historical significance. Explore the monastic life and cultural heritage.

20. Sant Sadurni d'Anoia:
   - Overview: Sant Sadurni d'Anoia, the heart of Catalonia's cava (sparkling wine) production region, offers a delightful day trip for wine enthusiasts. Take guided tours of cava cellars, learn about the wine-making process, and indulge in tastings of exquisite Catalan sparkling wine.

21. Catalan Pyrenees:
   - Overview: The Catalan Pyrenees, located within a few hours of Barcelona, present a spectacular natural setting. This mountain range is ideal for outdoor enthusiasts, offering opportunities for hiking, skiing in the winter, and experiencing the beauty of the Pyrenees.

Each of these day trip destinations from Barcelona has its own distinct appeal, whether you're interested in art and culture, history, nature, or simply enjoying the regional cuisine and wines. Catalonia's diverse landscapes and rich heritage make it an ideal region to explore beyond the city of Barcelona, offering an array of memorable day trip experiences.

11. Practical Information

- Currency and banking

Here is some extensive information on currency and banking in Barcelona:

- The official currency of Spain is the euro (EUR), which is divided into 100 cents. There are coins of 1, 2, 5, 10, 20 and 50 cents, and 1 and 2 euros. There are banknotes of 5, 10, 20, 50, 100, 200 and 500 euros.

- Currency and traveler's checks can be changed at all the local airports. When you get to Barcelona, it's best to exchange currency or traveler's checks at a bank, not a cambio (exchange bureau), hotel, or shop as rates and commission fees are high. Most Barcelona hotels accept major credit and debit cards.

- To open a non-resident's account in Spain, all you need is your passport, or your non-resident NIE and photo ID. However, not all banks offer non-resident accounts. If you have your resident NIE, legally you should open a resident's bank account. To open this type of account you will be asked to show your resident NIE (or TIE if you're from the UK or any other country not in the EU) photo ID, an address in Spain, a contact telephone number, email, and your employment or work details.

- Some of the best banks in Spain that offer free banking are Open Bank, N26, ING, and Wise. These are online banks that provide basic banking features such as current accounts, debit cards, money transfers, and customer service. Some of them also offer extra services such as travel insurance, car rental insurance, mobile phone insurance, and customer offers for a monthly fee.

- If your bank has an international partner with a local bank in Barcelona, you might be able to withdraw money from their ATMs for free or for a reduced ATM fee. It's a good idea to check with your home bank whether they have any partnerships before you leave for Barcelona. At the same time, notify your bank that you'll be travelling to avoid having your card suspended while using it out of the country.

- When withdrawing EUR from an ATM in Barcelona, always choose to be charged in the local currency. Allowing the ATM to charge you in your home currency means they'll apply a poorer exchange rate and charge extra fees for their service. This question may be worded differently - whether you wish to withdraw money with or without conversion. Choose to continue without conversion as you want the transaction to be charged in EUR.

I hope this information helps you with your travel plans. Have a wonderful time in Barcelona! ●.

  - Language
In Barcelona, the following languages are commonly spoken and recognized:

1. Catalan (Català): Catalan is the dominant language in Barcelona and the Catalonia region. It's the primary language of instruction in schools, used in government and administration, and widely spoken in daily life.

2. Spanish (Castilian): Spanish is the second official language in Catalonia and is widely spoken and understood in Barcelona. Most people in the city are bilingual in Catalan and Spanish.

3. English: English is commonly spoken in the tourism industry, with many people working in hotels, restaurants, and tourist attractions proficient in English. Menus, signage, and information in English are readily available, especially in tourist areas.

4. Other European Languages: Due to the city's popularity as a tourist destination, you may encounter people who have basic knowledge of other European languages such as French, German, and Italian. However, English is the most commonly spoken non-native language.

Barcelona's linguistic diversity, with Catalan as the primary language and Spanish as a significant second language, contributes to the unique cultural experience of the city.

Catalan Simple Phrases to know.
When visiting Barcelona, learning some basic Catalan phrases can be a respectful and enriching way to engage

with the local culture. Here are some common Catalan phrases and words to get you started:

1. Greetings:
   - "Hola" - Hello
   - "Bon dia" - Good morning
   - "Bona tarda" - Good afternoon
   - "Bona nit" - Good night

2. Common Phrases:
   - "Si us plau" - Please
   - "Gràcies" - Thank you
   - "De res" - You're welcome
   - "Perdó" - Excuse me / Sorry
   - "Adéu" - Goodbye
   - "Com et dius?" - What's your name?
   - "No entenc" - I don't understand
   - "Parles anglès?" - Do you speak English?

3. Numbers:
   - "Zero" - Zero
   - "Un" - One
   - "Dos" - Two
   - "Tres" - Three
   - "Quatre" - Four
   - "Cinc" - Five
   - "Sis" - Six
   - "Set" - Seven
   - "Vuit" - Eight
   - "Nou" - Nine
   - "Deu" - Ten

4. Directions and Places:
   - "On és el bany?" - Where is the bathroom?
   - "Una taula per a dos" - A table for two
   - "L'estació de tren" - The train station
   - "L'aeroport" - The airport
   - "La platja" - The beach
   - "El museu" - The museum

5. Food and Dining:
   - "Una taula per a dos" - A table for two
   - "La carta" - The menu
   - "Vull això, sisplau" - I want this, please
   - "El compte" - The bill

6. Shopping:
   - "Quanto costa això?" - How much does this cost?
   - "Vull comprar aquest/aquesta." - I want to buy this.
   - "Té aquest/aquesta en una mida diferent?" - Do you have this in a different size?
   - "Pot donar-me un descompte?" - Can you give me a discount?

7. Emergencies:
   - "Ajuda!" - Help!
   - "Truqueu a la policia" - Call the police.
   - "Necessito un metge" - I need a doctor.
   - "On és l'hospital més proper?" - Where is the nearest hospital?

8. Common Expressions:

- "No tinc pressa" - I'm not in a hurry.
- "Em dic..." - My name is...
- "Estic de vacances" - I'm on vacation.
- "Benvingut/da" - Welcome.

9. Transportation:
   - "Una targeta de transport" - A transportation card.
   - "Quan parteix el pròxim tren/bus?" - When does the next train/bus depart?
   - "Em puc acomiadar aquí?" - Can I get off here?
   - "Estació d'autobusos" - Bus station.
   - "Estació de tren" - Train station.

10. Time and Dates:
   - "Quina hora és?" - What time is it?
   - "Avui és..." - Today is...
   - "Demà" - Tomorrow.
   - "Ahir" - Yesterday.
   - "Setmana" - Week.
   - "Mes" - Month.
   - "Any" - Year.

Learning and using these basic Catalan phrases can enhance your experience in Barcelona, as it shows respect for the local culture and language. Most people in Barcelona are bilingual in both Catalan and Spanish, so they will often switch to Spanish or English to assist you if needed.

Spanish Simple Phrases to know.

While Catalan is the primary language in Barcelona, many people are bilingual and understand Spanish. Learning some common Spanish phrases can also be very helpful during your visit. Here are some basic Spanish phrases to get you started:

1. Greetings:
   - "Hola" - Hello
   - "Buenos días" - Good morning
   - "Buenas tardes" - Good afternoon
   - "Buenas noches" - Good evening / Good night

2. Common Phrases:
   - "Por favor" - Please
   - "Gracias" - Thank you
   - "De nada" - You're welcome
   - "Perdón" - Excuse me / Sorry
   - "Adiós" - Goodbye
   - "¿Cómo te llamas?" - What's your name?
   - "No entiendo" - I don't understand
   - "¿Hablas inglés?" - Do you speak English?

3. Numbers:
   - "Cero" - Zero
   - "Uno" - One
   - "Dos" - Two
   - "Tres" - Three
   - "Cuatro" - Four
   - "Cinco" - Five
   - "Seis" - Six
   - "Siete" - Seven

- "Ocho" - Eight
- "Nueve" - Nine
- "Diez" - Ten

4. Directions and Places:
   - "¿Dónde está el baño?" - Where is the bathroom?
   - "Una mesa para dos" - A table for two
   - "La estación de tren" - The train station
   - "El aeropuerto" - The airport
   - "La playa" - The beach
   - "El museo" - The museum

5. Food and Dining:
   - "La carta" - The menu
   - "Quiero esto, por favor" - I want this, please
   - "La cuenta" - The bill
   - "El menú del día" - The daily special menu
   - "Una botella de agua" - A bottle of water
   - "Un café" - A coffee

6. Shopping:
   - "¿Cuánto cuesta esto?" - How much does this cost?
   - "Quiero comprar esto/esta." - I want to buy this.
   - "Tiene esto/esta en una talla diferente?" - Do you have this in a different size?
   - "¿Puede darme un descuento?" - Can you give me a discount?

7. Emergencies:
   - "Ayuda" - Help
   - "Llame a la policía" - Call the police

- "Necesito un médico" - I need a doctor
- "¿Dónde está el hospital más cercano?" - Where is the nearest hospital?

8. Common Expressions:
   - "No tengo prisa" - I'm not in a hurry
   - "Me llamo..." - My name is...
   - "Estoy de vacaciones" - I'm on vacation
   - "Bienvenido/a" - Welcome

9. Transportation:
   - "Un billete de transporte" - A transportation ticket
   - "¿Cuándo sale el próximo tren/bus?" - When does the next train/bus leave?
   - "¿Puedo bajar aquí?" - Can I get off here?
   - "Estación de autobuses" - Bus station
   - "Estación de tren" - Train station

10. Time and Dates:
   - "¿Qué hora es?" - What time is it?
   - "Hoy es..." - Today is...
   - "Mañana" - Tomorrow
   - "Ayer" - Yesterday
   - "Semana" - Week
   - "Mes" - Month
   - "Año" - Year

These Spanish phrases will certainly come in handy as you explore Barcelona. Many locals in Barcelona, especially in the tourist industry, are accustomed to conversing in Spanish and English, so you'll find these phrases to be valuable during your stay.

- Emergency numbers
Here is some extensive information on emergency numbers in Barcelona:

- The main emergency number for all kinds of situations is 112. You can call this number for free from any phone and get assistance in different languages, including English, Spanish, Catalan, French, German, and Italian.
- The other emergency numbers for specific services are:
    - 061 for medical emergencies and ambulances.
    - 080 for fire service and fire brigade.
    - 092 or 091 for local police or Policia Local. They are responsible for public order, traffic safety and control, and neighborhood disputes.
    - 088 for Catalan regional police or Mossos d'Esquadra. They are responsible for crime investigations, crime prevention, and assistance at accident scenes.
    - 091 for national Spanish police or Policia Nacional. They handle criminal, judicial, terrorism, and immigration matters in Spain, except in the Basque Country and Catalonia territories. They also issue DNI ID cards and passports.
    - 062 for civil guard or Guardia Civil. They are a national Spanish police force with both military and civilian functions. They control customs and entry points into the country, such as airports and shipping ports.

- Some other useful numbers for Barcelona emergency services are:
  - 902 111 444 for health rapid response line (24 hour).
  - 900 703 030 for social help center (24 hour).
  - 902 230 238 for office for non-discrimination.
  - 934 208 88 for special taxis for people with reduced mobility.
  - 933 043 118 for information about on duty chemists.
  - 934 208 088 for medicines night home delivery (only for subscribers).
  - 932 053 116, 608 893 555, 935 811 894, 934 268 746, 609 415 656, or 932 057 238 for veterinary surgeons (24 hours).
- For international calls, you need to dial the country code (34) followed by the nine-digit number. To call from Barcelona internationally, dial 00, then the country code, city code, and number. Calling overseas from a pay phone is very expensive. You may want to buy a prepaid long distance/international calling card.
- For consulates of different countries in Barcelona, you can find their addresses and phone numbers on this website: [Consulates in Barcelona](https://www.barcelona.com/barcelona_city_guide/all_about/useful_numbers/consulates). Some examples are:
  - United Kingdom: Av. Diagonal, 477, 13º 08036 Barcelona (+34)933666200
  - Canada: Elisenda Pinós, 10 08034 Barcelona (+34)932042700
  - United States of America: Paseo Reina Elisenda de Montcada, 23 08034 Barcelona (+34)933877077

I hope this information is helpful to you.. ●

- Travel tips and safety.
Barcelona is a beautiful and vibrant city that attracts millions of visitors every year. However, like any big city, it also has some risks and challenges that you should be aware of before you travel. Here are some extensive tips and advice on how to stay safe and enjoy your trip to Barcelona:

- Be careful of pickpockets and scammers. Barcelona is notorious for having a high rate of petty theft, especially in crowded and touristy areas such as La Rambla, El Raval, the Gothic Quarter, and the metro. Pickpockets often work in teams and use distraction techniques to steal your valuables. Some common scams include:
   - The bird poop scam: Someone splashes a liquid on you (pretending it's bird poop) and then offers to help you clean it, while another person steals your belongings.
   - The rose scam: A woman offers you a rose or a bracelet for free, but then demands money or tries to snatch your wallet or bag.
   - The gaming scam: You see a table with people playing a game of chance, such as the shell game or the three-card monte. They invite you to join and bet money, but the game is rigged and you will always lose.
   - The petition scam: Someone asks you to sign a petition for a good cause, but then asks for a donation or

tries to distract you while another person steals from you.

- The fake police scam: Someone approaches you and claims to be a police officer. They ask to see your passport or wallet, and then either take it or switch it with a fake one.

- The metro scam: Someone bumps into you or blocks your way in the metro, while another person picks your pocket or bag.

- To avoid falling victim to these scams, you should:

- Keep your valuables in a secure place, such as a money belt, a hidden pocket, or a locked backpack. Don't carry your wallet in a back pocket or put your phone or camera on tables at cafes.

- Be alert and vigilant in public places, especially when someone approaches you or tries to get your attention. Don't let anyone touch you or your belongings without your consent.

- Don't accept anything for free from strangers, such as flowers, bracelets, flyers, or CDs. Politely decline and walk away.

- Don't play any games of chance on the street. They are always scams and you will lose your money.

- Don't sign any petitions or give any donations to strangers. If you want to support a cause, do some research and find a reputable organization.

- Don't show your passport or wallet to anyone who claims to be a police officer. Ask for their identification and badge number, and call the real police if you have any doubts.

- Be careful when entering and exiting the metro. Hold your bag in front of you and don't let anyone block your way. If someone bumps into you, check your pockets and bag immediately.

- Know the emergency numbers and how to use them. In case of an emergency, such as a medical issue, a fire, an accident, or a crime, you should know how to contact the appropriate authorities and services. The main emergency number for all kinds of situations is 112. You can call this number for free from any phone and get assistance in different languages, including English, Spanish, Catalan, French, German, and Italian. The other emergency numbers for specific services are:
   - 061 for medical emergencies and ambulances.
   - 080 for fire service and fire brigade.
   - 092 or 091 for local police or Policia Local. They are responsible for public order, traffic safety and control, and neighborhood disputes.
   - 088 for Catalan regional police or Mossos d'Esquadra. They are responsible for crime investigations, crime prevention, and assistance at accident scenes.
   - 091 for national Spanish police or Policia Nacional. They handle criminal, judicial, terrorism, and immigration matters in Spain, except in the Basque Country and Catalonia territories. They also issue DNI ID cards and passports.
   - 062 for civil guard or Guardia Civil [^4^. They are a national Spanish police force with both military and civilian functions. They control customs and entry

points into the country, such as airports and shipping ports.
-Other Emergency contacts are mentioned above.

- Follow the local laws and customs. Barcelona is a cosmopolitan and tolerant city, but it also has its own culture and traditions that you should respect and appreciate. Some things to keep in mind are:

  - Barcelona is the capital of Catalonia, a region that has a distinct identity, history, and language from the rest of Spain. Many Catalans feel strongly about their autonomy and independence, and some may not appreciate being called Spanish or being spoken to in Spanish. The official languages of Catalonia are Catalan and Spanish, but most people also speak English. You may want to learn some basic phrases in Catalan, such as "bon dia" (good day), "gràcies" (thank you), and "adéu" (goodbye), to show your respect and interest.

  - Barcelona is a city of art and architecture, with many famous landmarks and monuments that are protected by law. You should not touch, climb, or vandalize any of these structures, as you may face fines or legal consequences. You should also be careful when taking photos or videos of these sites, as some may require permission or a fee. You can check the official websites of the attractions for more information.

  - Barcelona is a city of festivals and celebrations, with many events happening throughout the year. Some of the most popular ones are La Mercè (the patron saint festival in September), Sant Jordi (the day of the book and the rose in April), and La Diada (the national day of Catalonia in September). These occasions are a great opportunity to experience the local culture and traditions, such as the human towers (castells), the fire runs (correfocs), and the giant puppets (gegants). However, you should also be respectful and careful when participating or observing these activities, as they may involve large crowds, loud noises, fireworks, or fire.

- Barcelona is a city of nightlife and entertainment, with many bars, clubs, restaurants, and theaters to choose from. You can enjoy a variety of music, cuisine, and shows in this lively city. However, you should also be aware of some rules and etiquette when going out at night. For example:

 - The legal drinking age in Spain is 18. You may be asked to show your ID when buying alcohol or entering some venues.
 - Drinking alcohol in public places is illegal and may result in fines or confiscation of your drinks.
 - Smoking is banned in all indoor public places, such as bars, restaurants, cinemas, and public transport. You can only smoke outside or in designated areas.
 - The typical dinner time in Spain is between 9 pm and 11 pm. Many restaurants may not open until then or may close earlier than you expect. You may want to make a reservation or check the opening hours before you go.

- The typical clubbing time in Spain is between midnight and 6 am. Many clubs may not open until then or may charge an entrance fee that includes a drink. You may want to dress smartly and carry some cash with you.

I hope these tips is useful.

12. Itineraries

- Sample 1-day.

There are many possible ways to spend a day in Barcelona, depending on your interests and preferences. Here is one example of a day itinerary that covers some of the most iconic and popular attractions in the city:

- Start your day with a visit to the Sagrada Familia, the masterpiece of Antoni Gaudí and the symbol of Barcelona. This stunning basilica is still under construction, but you can admire its intricate façades and towers, as well as its awe-inspiring interior. You can also climb up one of the towers for a panoramic view of the city. Make sure to book your tickets online in advance to avoid long queues.

- Next, take the metro to Passeig de Gràcia, one of the most elegant boulevards in Barcelona. Here you can see some of Gaudí's other works, such as Casa Batlló and Casa Milà (also known as La Pedrera). These are two of the most famous examples of modernist architecture, with their colorful façades and organic shapes. You can also enter these buildings and explore their interiors, which are equally fascinating.

- For lunch, head to La Boqueria, the largest and most famous market in Barcelona. Here you can find a variety of fresh and delicious products, such as fruits, vegetables, cheese, meat, seafood, and more. You can also sample some of the local specialties, such as jamón ibérico (cured ham), pa amb tomàquet (bread with tomato), or croquetas (fried balls of béchamel sauce and different fillings). There are also many stalls and bars where you can enjoy a tapa (a small dish) or a pintxo (a bite-sized snack on a skewer) with a glass of wine or beer.

- After lunch, walk along Las Ramblas, the most famous street in Barcelona. This is a lively and bustling avenue that connects Plaça de Catalunya with the port. Along the way, you can see street performers, artists, flower vendors, and souvenir shops. You can also stop by some of the landmarks along Las Ramblas, such as the Gran Teatre del Liceu (the opera house), the Palau de la Virreina (a cultural center), or the Font de Canaletes (a fountain where football fans celebrate their victories) .

- At the end of Las Ramblas, you will reach the Monument a Colom (the Columbus Monument), a 60-meter-high statue that commemorates the explorer's first voyage to America. From here, you can take a short walk to the Barceloneta Beach, one of the most popular beaches in Barcelona. Here you can relax on the sand, swim in the sea, or enjoy some water sports. You can also find many bars and restaurants along the beachfront, where you can have a drink or a snack while watching the sunset .

- For dinner, head to El Born, one of the oldest and most charming neighborhoods in Barcelona. This area is full of narrow streets, medieval buildings, and hidden squares. It is also home to many trendy shops, galleries, and cafes. Here you can find some of the best restaurants in Barcelona, offering a variety of cuisines, from traditional Catalan to fusion to international. You can also try some of the local dishes, such as fideuà (a paella-like dish with noodles), escalivada (roasted vegetables), or crema catalana (a custard dessert)[^1] [^2] .

- To end your day in style, go to Palau de la Música Catalana, one of the most beautiful concert halls in the world. This stunning building was designed by Lluís Domènech i Montaner, another modernist architect. It features a colorful façade, a spectacular stained glass ceiling, and a richly decorated interior. You can either take a guided tour of the building or attend one of the concerts that are held regularly[^1] [^2] .

This is just one possible way to spend a day in Barcelona. There are many other attractions and activities that you can choose from, depending on your interests and time. You can use this website to find more information and tips about Barcelona. I hope you enjoy your stay in this amazing city!

 -Sample 3-days.
Here is a sample itinerary for 3 days in Barcelona, based on the web search results I found. You can use this as a reference or modify it according to your preferences.

Day 1: Explore the historic center of Barcelona and admire some of Gaudí's masterpieces. You can visit the following places:

- Casa Batlló: Admire one of Gaudí's most iconic works, with its colorful façade and organic shapes. You can also enter the building and explore its interior, which is equally fascinating.

- Barcelona History Museum: Learn about the history and culture of Barcelona from its origins to the present day. You can also see the remains of the Roman city under the Gothic Quarter.

- Taperia Princesa: Enjoy some of the best tapas in Barcelona at this cozy and authentic restaurant in El Born. You can also try some of the local dishes, such as fideuà, escalivada, or crema catalana.

- Picasso Museum: See one of the largest and most comprehensive collections of Picasso's works, especially from his early years and his Blue Period. You can also admire some of his paintings inspired by Las Meninas by Velázquez.

- La Boqueria Market: Taste some of the fresh and delicious products at the largest and most famous market in Barcelona. You can also sample some of the local specialties, such as jamón ibérico, pa amb tomàquet, or croquetas.

- Flamenco Dance Show: Enjoy a traditional Spanish dance performance at one of the many venues in Barcelona. You can also have dinner or a drink while watching the show.

- Sagrada Familia: Marvel at Gaudí's masterpiece and symbol of Barcelona, a stunning basilica that is still under construction. You can admire its intricate façades and towers, as well as its awe-inspiring interior. You can also climb up one of the towers for a panoramic view of the city. Make sure to book your tickets online in advance to avoid long queues.

- Bunkers del Carmel: Climb up to the top of Turó de la Rovira, where you can see the remains of an anti-aircraft battery from the Spanish Civil War. You can also admire a stunning 360-degree view of Barcelona from this vantage point.

- El Born: Walk around one of the oldest and most charming neighborhoods in Barcelona, full of narrow streets, medieval buildings, and hidden squares. It is also home to many trendy shops, galleries, and cafes.

Day 2: Visit some of the most famous landmarks and attractions in Barcelona, such as Parc Güell, Las Ramblas, and Barceloneta Beach. You can visit the following places:

- Parc Güell: Discover one of Gaudí's most whimsical creations, a park full of colorful mosaics, sculptures, and buildings. You can also enjoy a panoramic view of the city from the main terrace.

- Casa Milà (also known as La Pedrera): See another example of Gaudí's modernist architecture, with its wavy façade and rooftop sculptures. You can also visit the inside of the building, which houses a museum and an exhibition space.

- Palau Güell [^2^. Visit one of Gaudí's earliest works, a palace that was commissioned by his patron Eusebi Güell. You can see the impressive main hall, the ornate fireplace, and the rooftop chimneys.

- Park Guell[^1^. Relax in one of the most beautiful and oldest parks in Barcelona, where you can find a lake, a fountain, a zoo, and a parliament. You can also see some monuments, such as the Arc de Triomf and the Castell dels Tres Dragons.

- Raval[^1^. Explore one of the most diverse and vibrant neighborhoods in Barcelona, where you can find many cultural attractions, such as museums, libraries, theaters, and art galleries. You can also find some of the best nightlife spots in the city.

Day 3: Explore some of the places of interest in Barcelona, such as Palau de la Musica Catalana, Casa Vicens, and Montjuic. You can visit the following places:

- Palau de la Musica Catalana[^1^. Visit one of the most beautiful concert halls in the world, designed by Lluís Domènech i Montaner, another modernist architect. It features a colorful façade, a spectacular stained glass ceiling, and a richly decorated interior. You can either take a guided tour of the building or attend one of the concerts that are held regularly.
- Casa Vicens[^1^. See one of Gaudí's first works, a house that was inspired by Moorish and Oriental styles. You can also see some of his signature elements, such as ceramic tiles, ironwork, and natural motifs.

- Montjuic[^1^. Discover one of the largest and greenest parks in Barcelona, where you can find many attractions, such as botanical gardens, museums, monuments, and a castle.

- The Olympic facilities[^1^. See where some of the events of the 1992 Summer Olympics took place, such as the Olympic Stadium, the Palau Sant Jordi, and the Olympic Tower.

- Montjuic Castle[^1^. Visit an old fortress that overlooks the city and the sea. You can learn about its history and see some exhibitions inside. You can also enjoy a panoramic view of Barcelona from its ramparts.

- Tapas in Plaça Espanya and Magic Fountain: Enjoy some of the best tapas in Barcelona at one of the many bars and restaurants around Plaça Espanya. You can also watch the Magic Fountain show, a spectacular display of water, light, and music.

This is just one possible way to spend 3 days in Barcelona. There are many other attractions and activities that you can choose from, depending on your interests and time. You can use this website[3] to find more information and tips about Barcelona. I hope you enjoy your stay in this amazing city! ●.

　-Sample 1 week.
Here is a sample itinerary for one week in Barcelona, based on the web search results I found. You can use this as a reference or modify it according to your preferences.

Day 1: Explore the historic center of Barcelona and admire some of Gaudí's masterpieces. You can visit the following places:

- Santa Eulàlia Cathedral and the Gothic Quarter: See the impressive Gothic cathedral and wander around the medieval streets and squares of the old town.

- Las Ramblas: Stroll along the most famous avenue in Barcelona, where you can see street performers, artists, flower vendors, and souvenir shops.

- La Boqueria Market: Taste some of the fresh and delicious products at the largest and most famous market in Barcelona. You can also sample some of the local specialties, such as jamón ibérico, pa amb tomàquet, or croquetas.

- Casa Batlló: Admire one of Gaudí's most iconic works, with its colorful façade and organic shapes. You can also enter the building and explore its interior, which is equally fascinating.

- Casa Milà (also known as La Pedrera): See another example of Gaudí's modernist architecture, with its wavy façade and rooftop sculptures. You can also visit the inside of the building, which houses a museum and an exhibition space.

- Attend a flamenco show: Enjoy a traditional Spanish dance performance at one of the many venues in Barcelona. You can also have dinner or a drink while watching the show.

Day 2: Visit some of the most famous landmarks and attractions in Barcelona, such as Parc Güell, Sagrada Familia, and El Born. You can visit the following places:

- Parc Güell: Discover one of Gaudí's most whimsical creations, a park full of colorful mosaics, sculptures, and buildings. You can also enjoy a panoramic view of the city from the main terrace.

- Carmel Bunkers: Climb up to the top of Turó de la Rovira, where you can see the remains of an anti-aircraft battery from the Spanish Civil War. You can also admire a stunning 360-degree view of Barcelona from this vantage point.

- Sant Pau Recinte Modernista: Visit the largest Art Nouveau complex in the world, which used to be a hospital. You can see the beautiful façades and gardens, as well as the interior of some of the pavilions.

- Sagrada Familia: Marvel at Gaudí's masterpiece and symbol of Barcelona, a stunning basilica that is still under construction. You can admire its intricate façades and towers, as well as its awe-inspiring interior. You can also climb up one of the towers for a panoramic view of the city. Make sure to book your tickets online in advance to avoid long queues.

- El Born: Walk around one of the oldest and most charming neighborhoods in Barcelona, full of narrow streets, medieval buildings, and hidden squares. It is also home to many trendy shops, galleries, and cafes.

Day 3: Explore some of the places of interest in Barcelona, such as Plaça d'Espanya, Montjuïc Park, and Camp Nou. You can visit the following places:

- Plaça d'Espanya: See one of the largest and most impressive squares in Barcelona, where you can find two Venetian towers, a fountain, and a former bullring that is now a shopping center.

- MNAC (National Art Museum of Catalonia): Visit one of the most important museums in Barcelona, which houses a collection of Catalan art from different periods. You can also enjoy a great view of the city from its terrace.

- Montjuïc Park: Discover one of the largest and greenest parks in Barcelona, where you can find many attractions, such as botanical gardens, museums, monuments, and a castle.

- The Olympic facilities [^2^. See where some of the events of the 1992 Summer Olympics took place, such as the Olympic Stadium, the Palau Sant Jordi, and the Olympic Tower.

- Montjuïc Castle[^1^. Visit an old fortress that overlooks the city and the sea. You can learn about its history and see some exhibitions inside. You can also enjoy a panoramic view of Barcelona from its ramparts.

- Tapas in Plaça Espanya and Magic Fountain: Enjoy some of the best tapas in Barcelona at one of the many bars and restaurants around Plaça Espanya. You can also watch the Magic Fountain show, a spectacular display of water, light, and music.

Day 4: Walk along the coast of Barcelona and enjoy some of the best beaches and parks in the city. You can visit the following places:

- The Old Port: See where the history of Barcelona began, a port that dates back to Roman times. You can also find many attractions, such as museums, aquariums, cinemas, and restaurants.

- The Maritime Promenade: Stroll along the seafront, where you can see some of the most emblematic landmarks of Barcelona, such as the Columbus Monument, the W Hotel, and the Barceloneta neighborhood.

- The Olympic Port: See where some of the sailing events of the 1992 Summer Olympics took place, a modern port that is now a popular leisure area. You can also find many bars, clubs, restaurants, and beaches.

- Ciutadella Park: Relax in one of the most beautiful and oldest parks in Barcelona, where you can find a lake, a fountain, a zoo, and a parliament. You can also see some monuments, such as the Arc de Triomf and the Castell dels Tres Dragons.

- Santa Maria del Mar Basilica: Admire one of the finest examples of Catalan Gothic architecture, a majestic church that was built by the people of Barcelona in the 14th century.

Day 5: Have a fun day at Port Aventura, one of the best theme parks in Europe. You can enjoy the following attractions:

- Port Aventura Park: Experience an adventure in six different themed areas, such as Mediterrània, Polynesia, China, Mexico, Far West, and SesamoAventura. You can find many rides, shows, shops, and restaurants for all ages and tastes.

- Ferrari Land [^2^. Feel the thrill of speed and adrenaline in this unique park dedicated to Ferrari. You can find many attractions, such as roller coasters, simulators, exhibitions, and games related to the world of Formula 1.

- Caribe Aquatic Park[^1^. Cool off in this water park that recreates a Caribbean paradise. You can find many attractions, such as slides, pools, waterfalls, and tropical plants.

Day 6: Visit Montserrat, a natural park and a religious site that is one of the most emblematic places in Catalonia. You can do the following activities:

- Take a train or a car to Montserrat[^1^. Travel from Barcelona to Montserrat by train or by car. The train takes about an hour and leaves from Plaça Espanya station. The car takes about an hour and a half and you can park at Monistrol de Montserrat or at the monastery.

- Take a cable car or a rack railway to the monastery[^1^. Choose between two options to reach the monastery from Monistrol de Montserrat: a cable car or a rack railway. Both take about 15 minutes and offer stunning views of the mountain.

- Visit the monastery and see the Black Madonna[^1^. Explore one of the most important religious sites in Catalonia, where you can find a basilica, a museum, an art gallery, and a library. You can also see the Black Madonna (La Moreneta), a wooden statue of the Virgin Mary that is venerated by many pilgrims.

- Hike or take a funicular to Sant Joan or Santa Cova[^1^. Enjoy some of the best views of Montserrat by hiking or taking a funicular to Sant Joan or Santa Cova. Sant Joan is a chapel on top of the mountain that offers panoramic views of Catalonia. Santa Cova is a cave where legend says that some shepherds found an image of the Virgin Mary.

- Taste some local products and buy some souvenirs[^1^. Try some of the local products that are made in Montserrat, such as cheese, honey, jam, liqueur, or chocolate. You can also buy some souvenirs at one of the shops near the monastery.

Day 7: Discover the Costa Brava, one of the most beautiful coastlines in Spain. You can visit some of these places:

- Tossa de Mar[^1^. Visit one of the most charming and picturesque towns on the Costa Brava, with its medieval walls, castle, and beach. You can also see some of the works of Marc Chagall, who lived here for a while.

- Calella de Palafrugell: Enjoy one of the most beautiful and authentic fishing villages on the Costa Brava, with its white houses, coves, and pine trees. You can also walk along the Camí de Ronda, a coastal path that connects different beaches and towns.

- Begur: Explore one of the most elegant and cosmopolitan towns on the Costa Brava, with its colonial-style houses, castle, and viewpoints. You can also visit some of the nearby beaches, such as Aiguablava, Sa Riera, or Sa Tuna.

- Pals: Discover one of the best-preserved medieval villages in Catalonia, with its cobblestone streets, stone houses, and Gothic church. You can also see some of the rice fields that surround the village and produce the famous rice of Pals.

- Empúries: Visit one of the most important archaeological sites in Catalonia, where you can see the remains of a Greek and a Roman city. You can also admire the stunning views of the sea and the mountains from this location.

This is just one possible way to spend a day on the Costa Brava. There are many other places and activities that you can choose from, depending on your interests and time. You can use this website to find more information and tips about the Costa Brava. I hope you have a wonderful time in this amazing region! ●

13. Maps and Resources

- Maps of the city and key locations

Here are some maps and resources for Barcelona that I found using my web search tool:

- If you want to see an interactive map of the city, where you can find addresses, attractions, and directions, you can use this website: [Interactive Barcelona map](^1^).

- If you want to see a sightseeing map of Barcelona, where you can find some of the most intriguing cultural treasures, such as Gaudí's buildings, museums, and monuments, you can use this website: [Sightseeing Map of Barcelona](^2^).

- If you want to see a road map of Barcelona, where you can find the best routes and directions for driving or

cycling, you can use this website: [Barcelona Map & Directions](^3^).
- If you want to see a tourist map of Barcelona, where you can find the best hotels, restaurants, and sites recommended by Michelin, you can use this website: [MICHELIN Barcelona map](^4^).

I hope these maps and resources are helpful to you. ●.

(1) Maps of Barcelona - City maps of Barcelona - Tourist map of Barcelona. https://www.barcelona.com/barcelona_city_guide/all_about/maps_barcelona.

(2) Barcelona Map • Sightseeing Map of Barcelona for 2023. https://www.barcelona-life.com/map.

(3) Barcelona Map & Directions - MapQuest. https://www.mapquest.com/es/catalunya/barcelona-28 2314922.

(4) MICHELIN Barcelona map - ViaMichelin. https://www.viamichelin.com/web/Maps/Map-Barcelo na-08001-Barcelona-Spain.

- Useful websites and apps
There are many useful websites and apps that travelers need to know about when going to Barcelona. Here are some of the ones that I found using my web search tool:

- Barcelona: 10 Things Travelers Need to Know Before Visiting: This website offers essential travel tips for visiting Barcelona, such as when to go, what to see, what to book in advance, where to stay, tipping etiquette, and more. It also includes some recommendations for the best experiences in Barcelona, such as Sagrada Familia, Park Güell, Montjuïc Cable Car, Barcelona Pass, and Casa Batlló.

- Traveling to Barcelona for the First Time (19 Tips & Tricks): This website provides practical and no-nonsense advice for planning your first trip to Barcelona. It covers topics such as how much time you need, how to avoid the crowds, how to save money, how to get around, and what to do and see in Barcelona. It also features some of the best attractions and activities in Barcelona, such as Parc Güell, Las Ramblas, Barceloneta Beach, Port Aventura, Montserrat, and Costa Brava.

- Information for travelling to Spain: This is the official website of Spain tourism, where you can find all the information you need for traveling to Spain. You can find information about visa and passport requirements, customs regulations, money and currency exchange, security and health tips, weather and climate, transportation and accessibility, culture and gastronomy, and more. You can also find information about the different regions and destinations in Spain, including Barcelona.

- Barcelona travel - Lonely Planet: This is one of the most popular and trusted travel guides for Barcelona. You can find comprehensive and up-to-date information about the city's history, culture, attractions, activities, events, nightlife, shopping, dining, and more. You can also find maps, photos, videos, reviews, and recommendations from other travelers. You can also book your flights, hotels, tours, and tickets through this website.

- 22 Best Travel Apps Every Traveler Should Know About: This website lists some of the best travel apps that can help you with various aspects of your trip. Some of the apps are general and useful for any destination, such as Google Maps, Tripadvisor, Skyscanner, Airbnb, Uber, etc. Some of the apps are specific for Barcelona or Spain, such as TMB (for public transportation), Bicing (for shared bikes), Cabify (for ride-sharing), Duolingo (for learning Catalan), Barcelona Official Guide (for sightseeing), Miniguide (for local tips), etc.

I hope these websites and apps are helpful to you.

(1) Barcelona: 10 Things Travelers Need to Know Before Visiting. https://www.traveloffpath.com/barcelona-things-travelers-need-to-know-before-visiting/.

(2) Traveling to Barcelona for the First Time (19 Tips & Tricks). https://fullsuitcase.com/barcelona-travel-tips/.

(3) Information for travelling to Spain | spain.info.
https://www.spain.info/en/info/.

(4) Barcelona travel - Lonely Planet | Spain, Europe.
https://www.lonelyplanet.com/spain/barcelona.

(5) 22 Best Travel Apps Every Traveler Should Know
About - Leisure.
https://www.travelandleisure.com/travel-news/best-fre
e-travel-apps.

14. Conclusion

- Final thoughts on Barcelona.
Barcelona is a wonderful city that has a lot to offer to its visitors. It is a city of art, culture, history, and diversity. It is also a city of contrasts, where you can find modern and ancient, urban and natural, cosmopolitan and local. Barcelona is a city that will surprise you and enchant you with its beauty and charm.

Some of the final thoughts that I have about Barcelona are:

- I admire the creativity and genius of Gaudí, who left his mark on the city with his amazing works of architecture. His buildings are not only beautiful, but also innovative and functional. He was able to blend nature, geometry, and symbolism in his designs. Some of his most famous works are Sagrada Familia, Casa Batlló, Casa Milà, and Parc Güell .

- I enjoy the diversity and vibrancy of Barcelona's neighborhoods, each with its own character and charm. I like to explore the Gothic Quarter, where I can see the traces of the Roman and medieval past of the city. I also like to visit El Born, where I can find trendy shops, galleries, and cafes. I also like to relax in Ciutadella Park, where I can see a lake, a fountain, a zoo, and a parliament .

- I love the food and drink culture of Barcelona, where I can taste some of the best dishes and products in Spain. I like to visit La Boqueria Market, where I can find fresh and delicious fruits, vegetables, cheese, meat, seafood, and more. I also like to sample some of the local specialties, such as jamón ibérico, pa amb tomàquet, croquetas, fideuà, escalivada, or crema catalana . I also like to enjoy some tapas or pintxos with a glass of wine or beer at one of the many bars and restaurants in the city .

- I appreciate the art and culture scene of Barcelona, where I can find some of the most important museums and galleries in Spain. I like to visit the Picasso Museum, where I can see one of the largest and most comprehensive collections of Picasso's works . I also like to visit the MNAC (National Art Museum of Catalonia), where I can see a collection of Catalan art from different periods [^2^. I also like to visit the Palau de la Musica Catalana, where I can see one of the most beautiful concert halls in the world .

Barcelona is a city that has something for everyone. Whether you are interested in architecture, history, nature, or nightlife, you will find it in Barcelona. It is a city that will make you fall in love with it. I hope you have enjoyed this travel guide and that you will have a great time in Barcelona! ●

- Contact me at my Gmail.

joedane427@gmail.com

Acknowledgment

"I would like to express my heartfelt gratitude to all the individuals, businesses, and organizations in Barcelona who generously shared their insights, knowledge, and hospitality. This travel guide would not have been possible without their support and the unique experiences they provided. I extend my appreciation to the diverse and welcoming people of Barcelona, who make this city a remarkable destination. Thank you for opening the doors to your culture and city, and for making every visitor feel at home."

Printed in Great Britain
by Amazon

37753993R00109